Parade ™
(with fireworks)

Mike Cavallaro

image® COMICS PRESENTS

A

Shadowline™

PRODUCTION

Parade™
(with fireworks)

Mike Cavallaro - Art and Story
Scott Friedlander - Book Design
Kristen Simon - Editor
Jim Valentino - Publisher

Shadowline™

image®

www.shadowlinecomics.com

PARADE (WITH FIREWORKS). First Printing. Published by Image Comics, Inc. Office of publication: 1942 University Avenue, Suite 305, Berkeley, California 94704. Copyright © 2008 Mike Cavallaro. Originally published in single magazine form as PARADE (WITH FIREWORKS) #1 and #2. All rights reserved. PARADE (WITH FIREWORKS)™ (including all prominent characters featured herein), its logo and all character likenesses are trademarks of Mike Cavallaro, unless otherwise noted. Image Comics® and its logos are registered trademarks of Image Comics, Inc. Shadowline™ and its logos are trademarks of Shadowline, Inc. No part of this publication may be reproduced or transmitted, in any form or by any means (except for short excerpts for review purposes) without the express written permission of Mr. Cavallaro. All names, characters, events and locales in this publication are entirely fictional. Any resemblance to actual persons (living or dead), events or places, without satiric intent, is coincidental.
ISBN: 978-1-58240-995-5
PRINTED IN CHINA

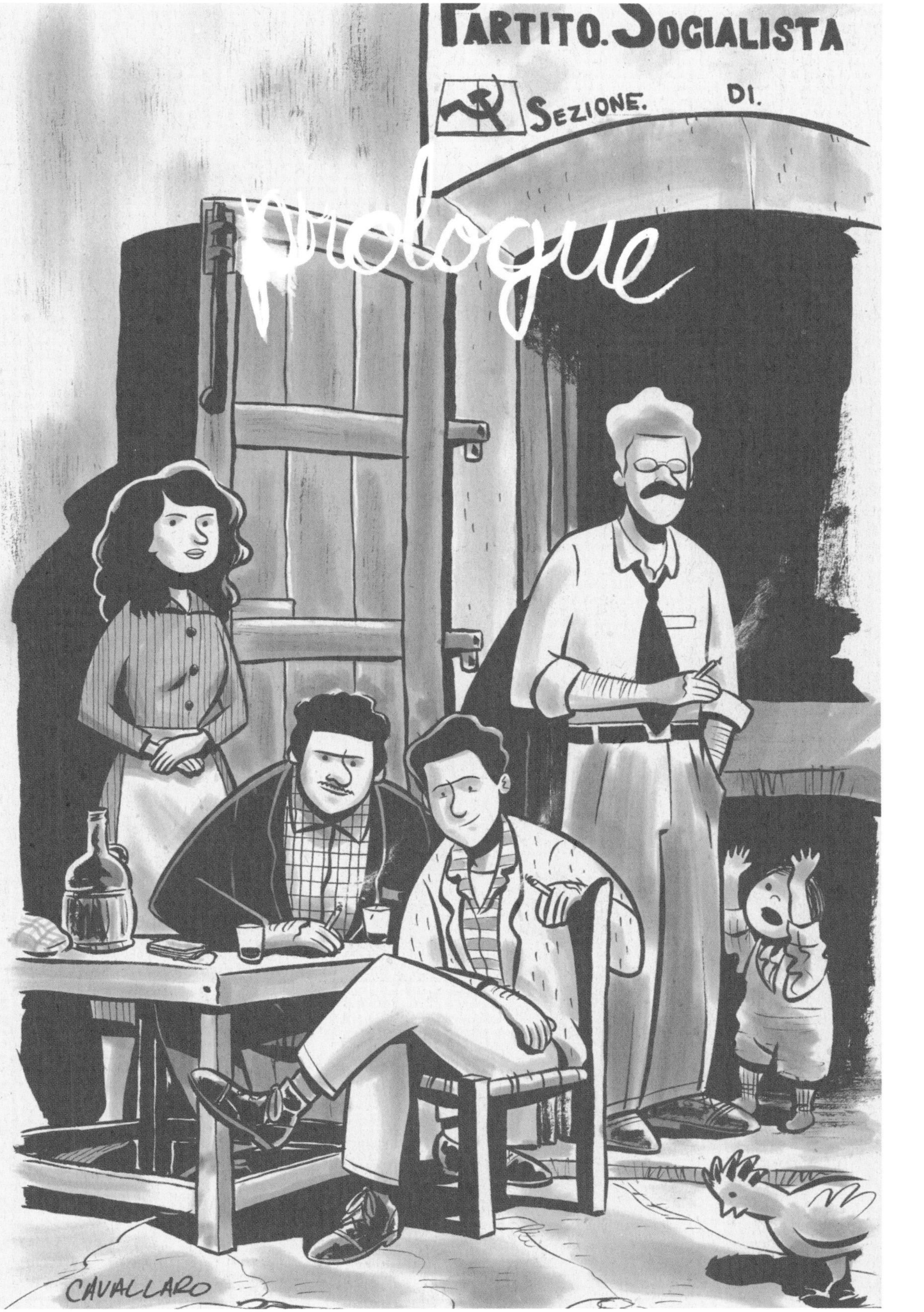
PARTITO. SOCIALISTA
SEZIONE. DI.
Prologue
CAVALLARO

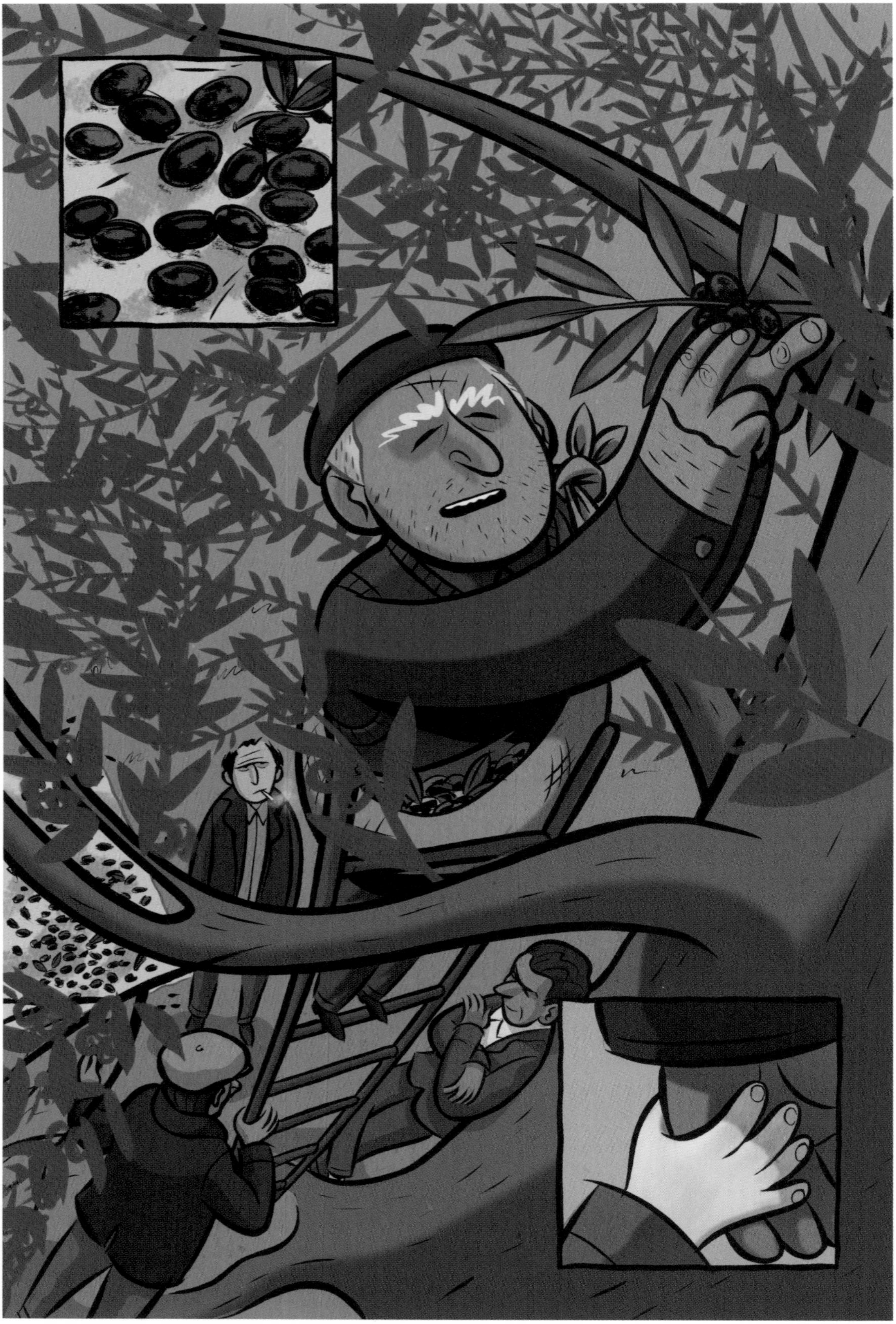

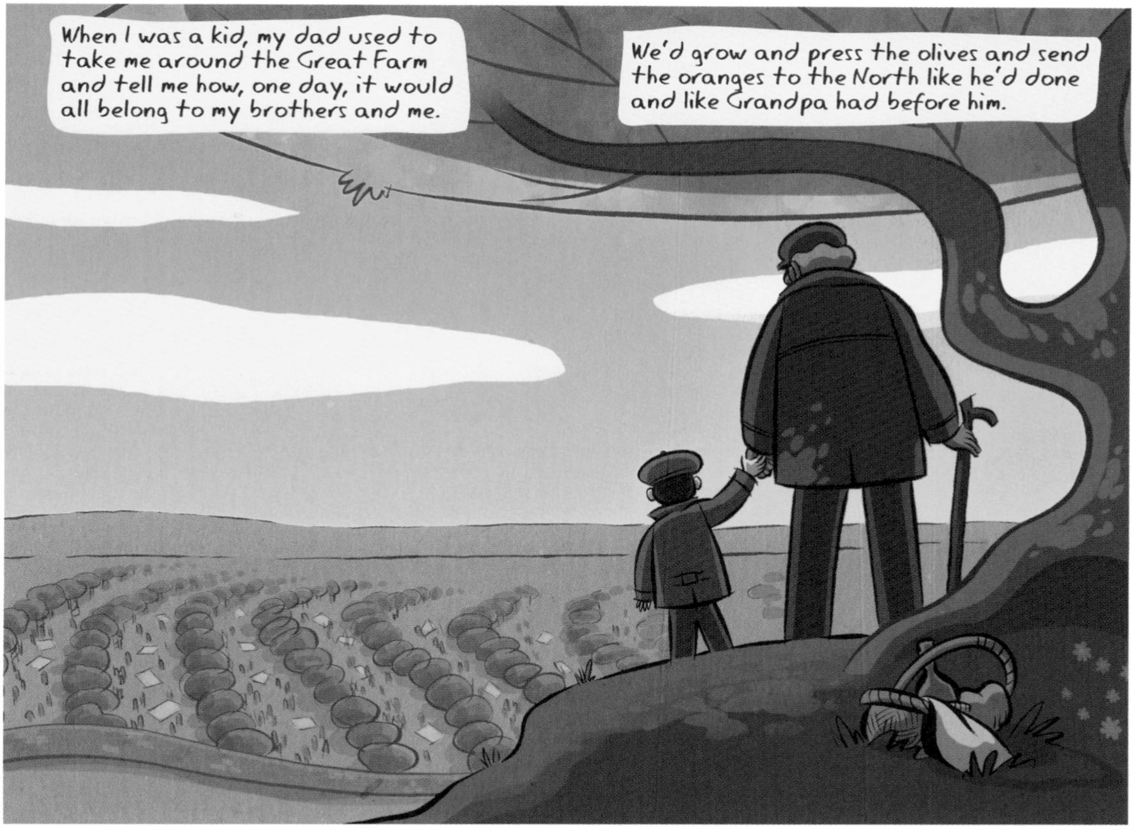
When I was a kid, my dad used to take me around the Great Farm and tell me how, one day, it would all belong to my brothers and me.
We'd grow and press the olives and send the oranges to the North like he'd done and like Grandpa had before him.

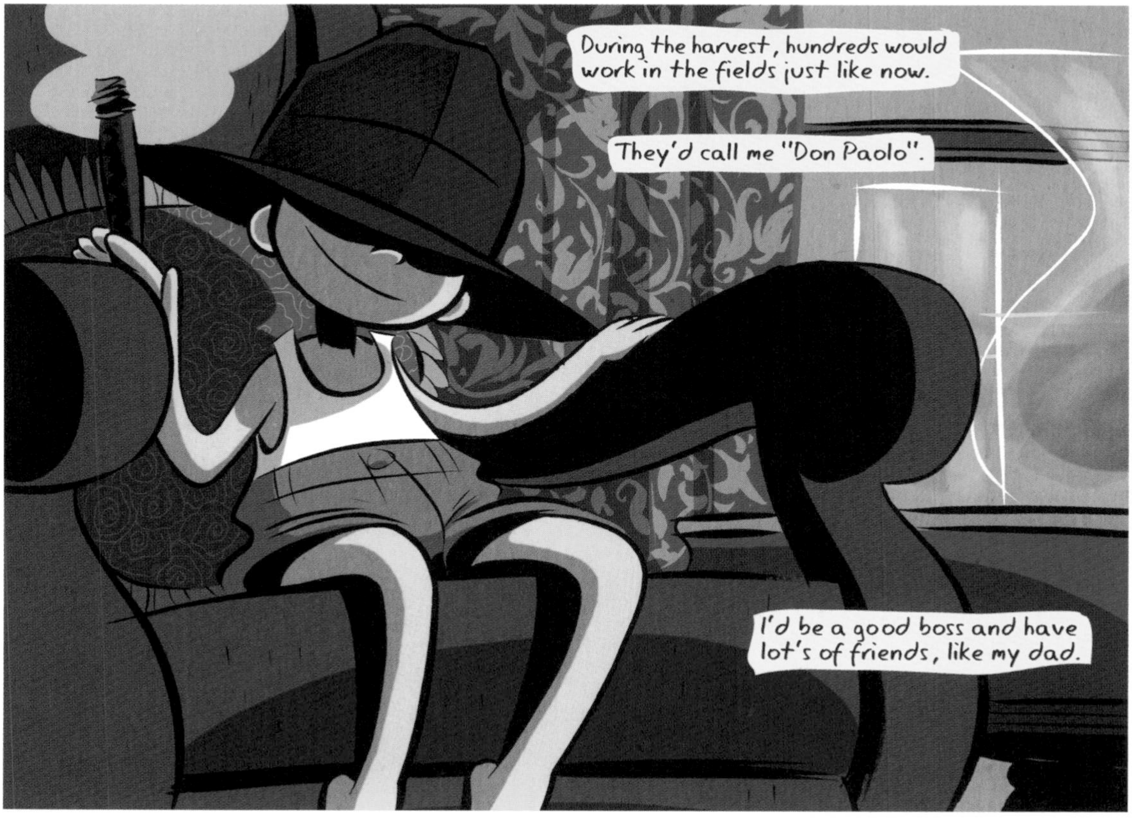
During the harvest, hundreds would work in the fields just like now.
They'd call me "Don Paolo".
I'd be a good boss and have lot's of friends, like my dad.

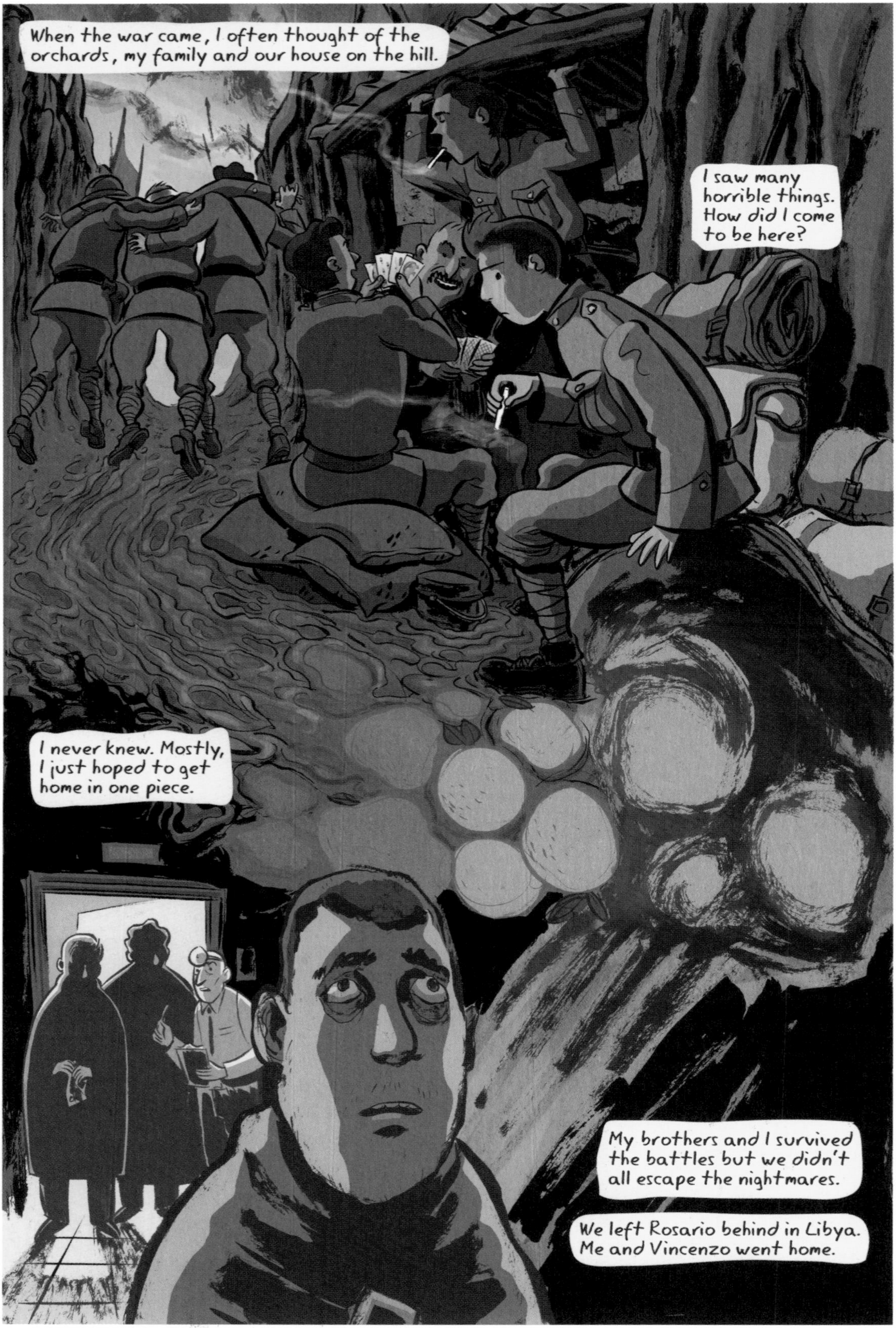
When the war came, I often thought of the orchards, my family and our house on the hill.
I saw many horrible things. How did I come to be here?
I never knew. Mostly, I just hoped to get home in one piece.
My brothers and I survived the battles but we didn't all escape the nightmares.
We left Rosario behind in Libya. Me and Vincenzo went home.

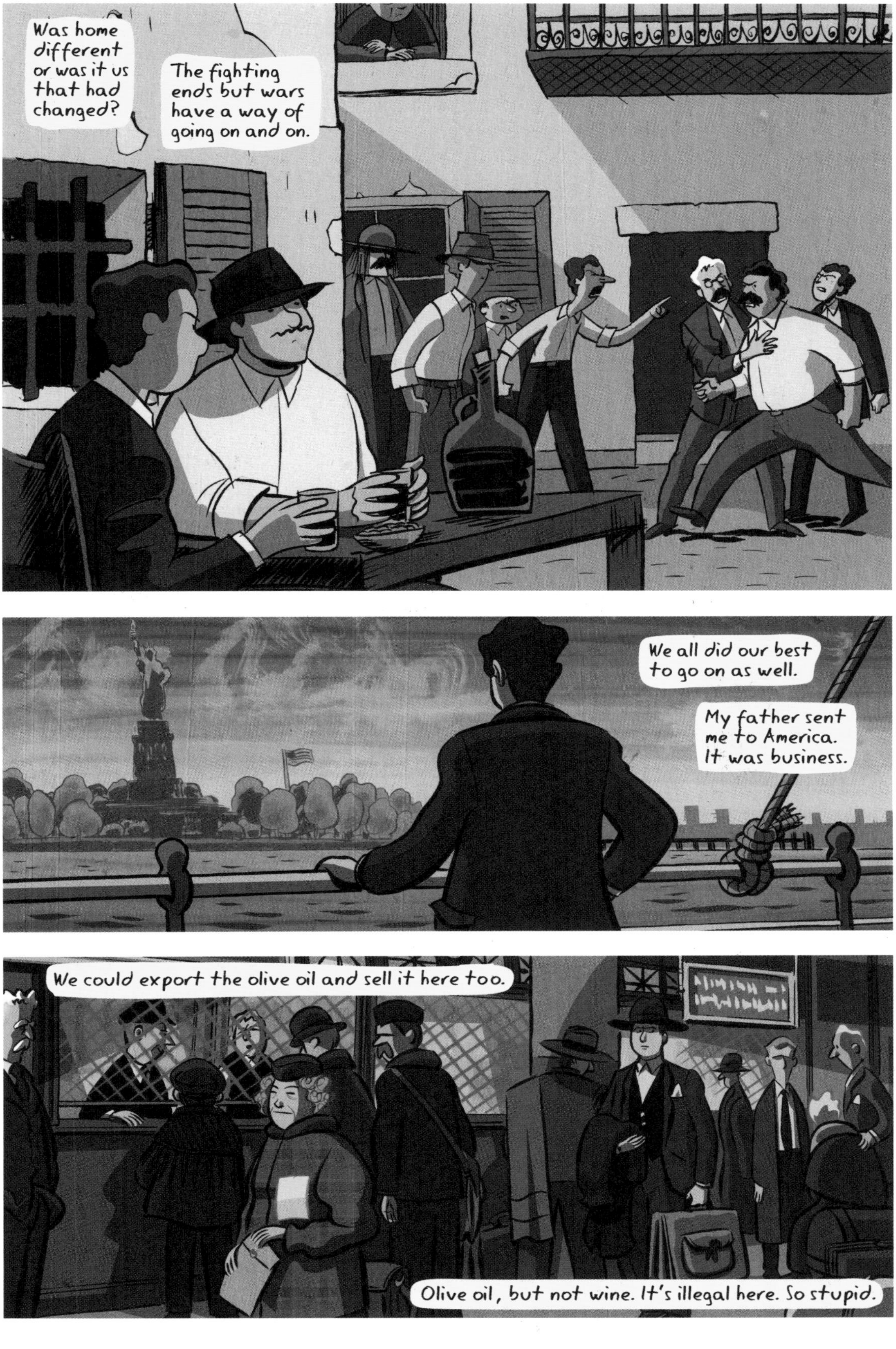
Was home different or was it us that had changed?
The fighting ends but wars have a way of going on and on.
We all did our best to go on as well.
My father sent me to America. It was business.
We could export the olive oil and sell it here too.
Olive oil, but not wine. It's illegal here. So stupid.

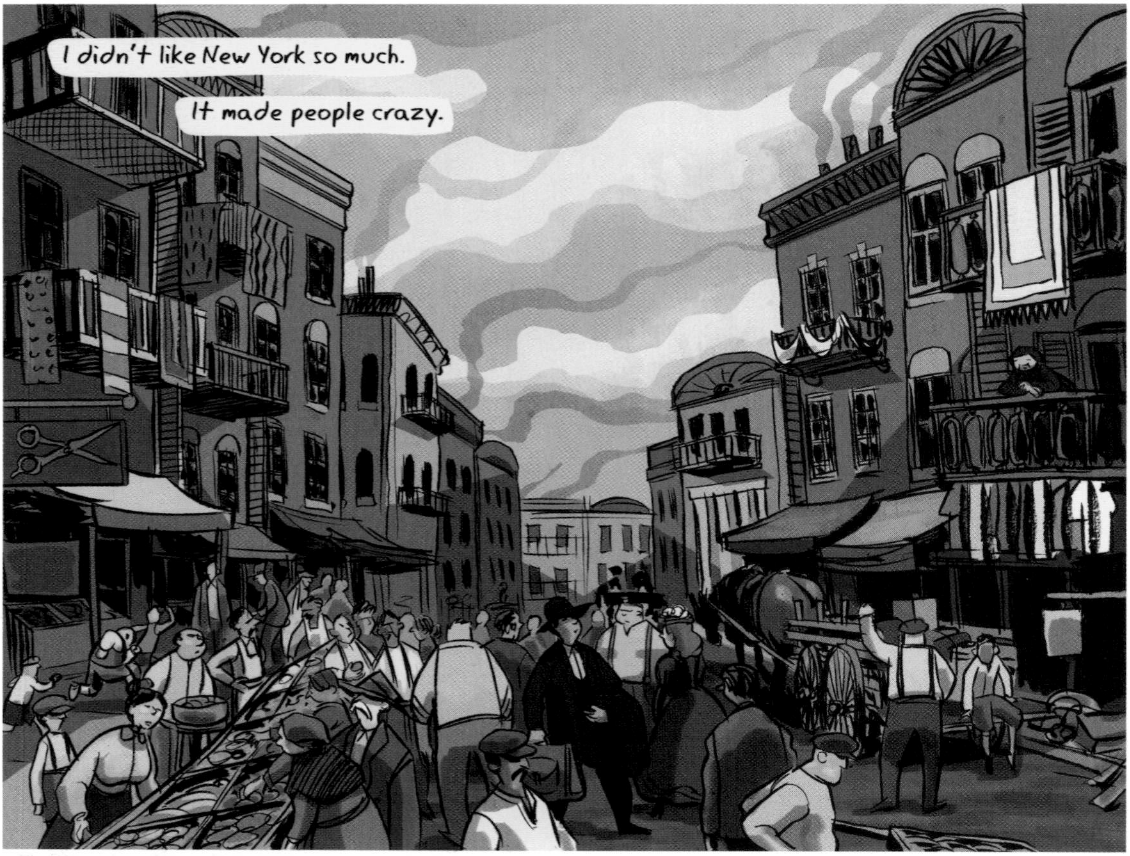
I didn't like New York so much.
It made people crazy.

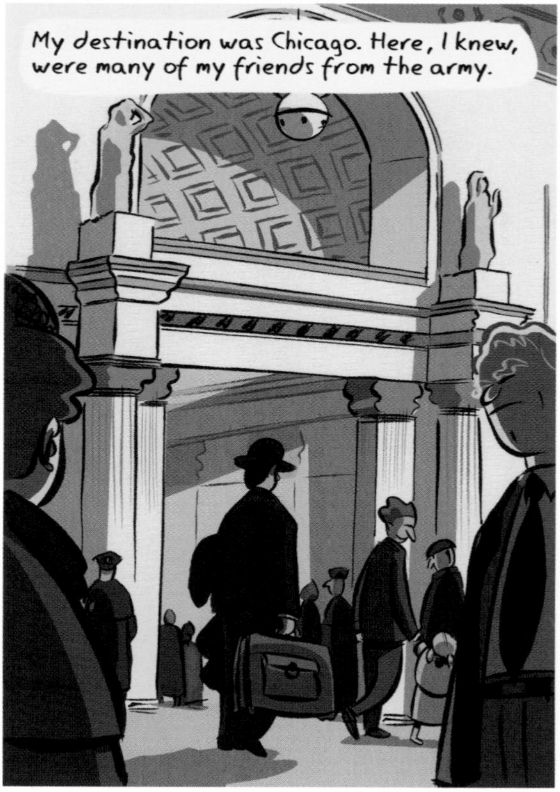
My destination was Chicago. Here, I knew, were many of my friends from the army.

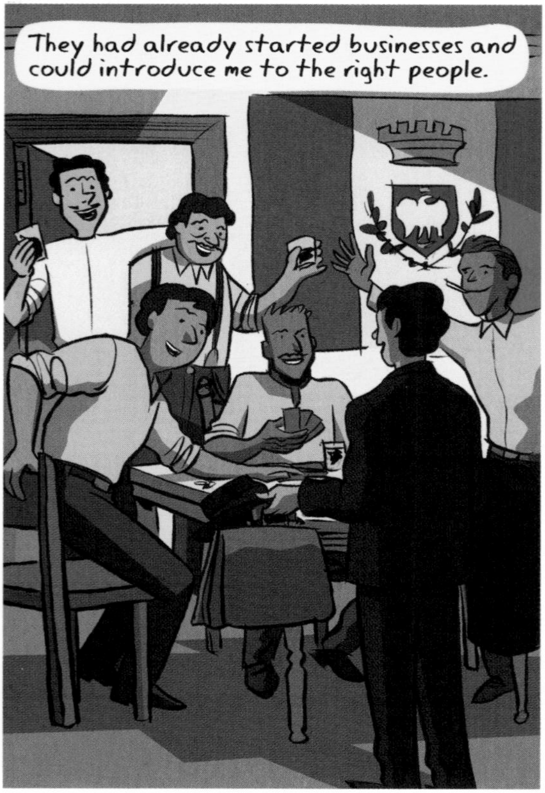
They had already started businesses and could introduce me to the right people.

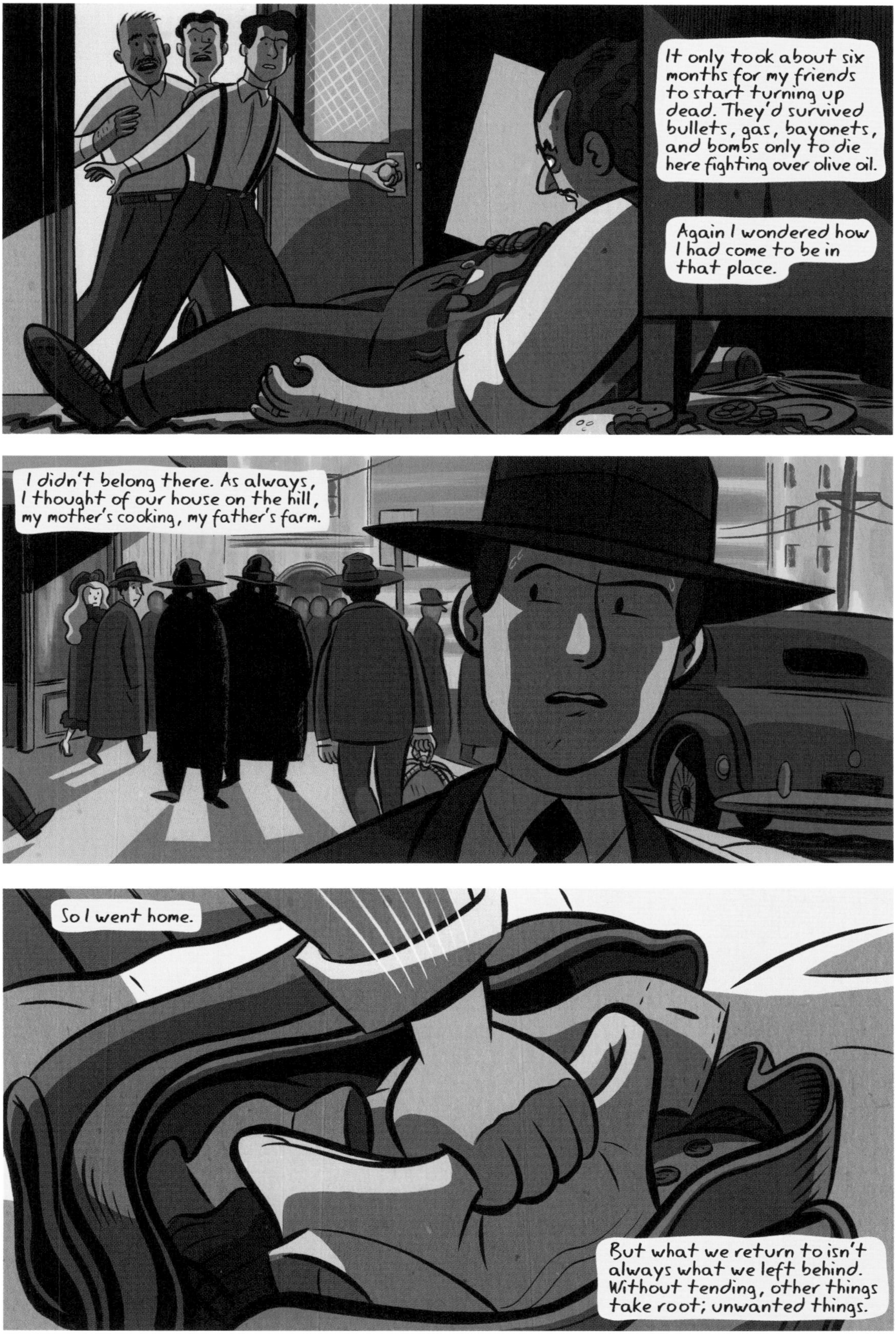
It only took about six months for my friends to start turning up dead. They'd survived bullets, gas, bayonets, and bombs only to die here fighting over olive oil.
Again I wondered how I had come to be in that place.
I didn't belong there. As always, I thought of our house on the hill, my mother's cooking, my father's farm.
So I went home.
But what we return to isn't always what we left behind. Without tending, other things take root; unwanted things.

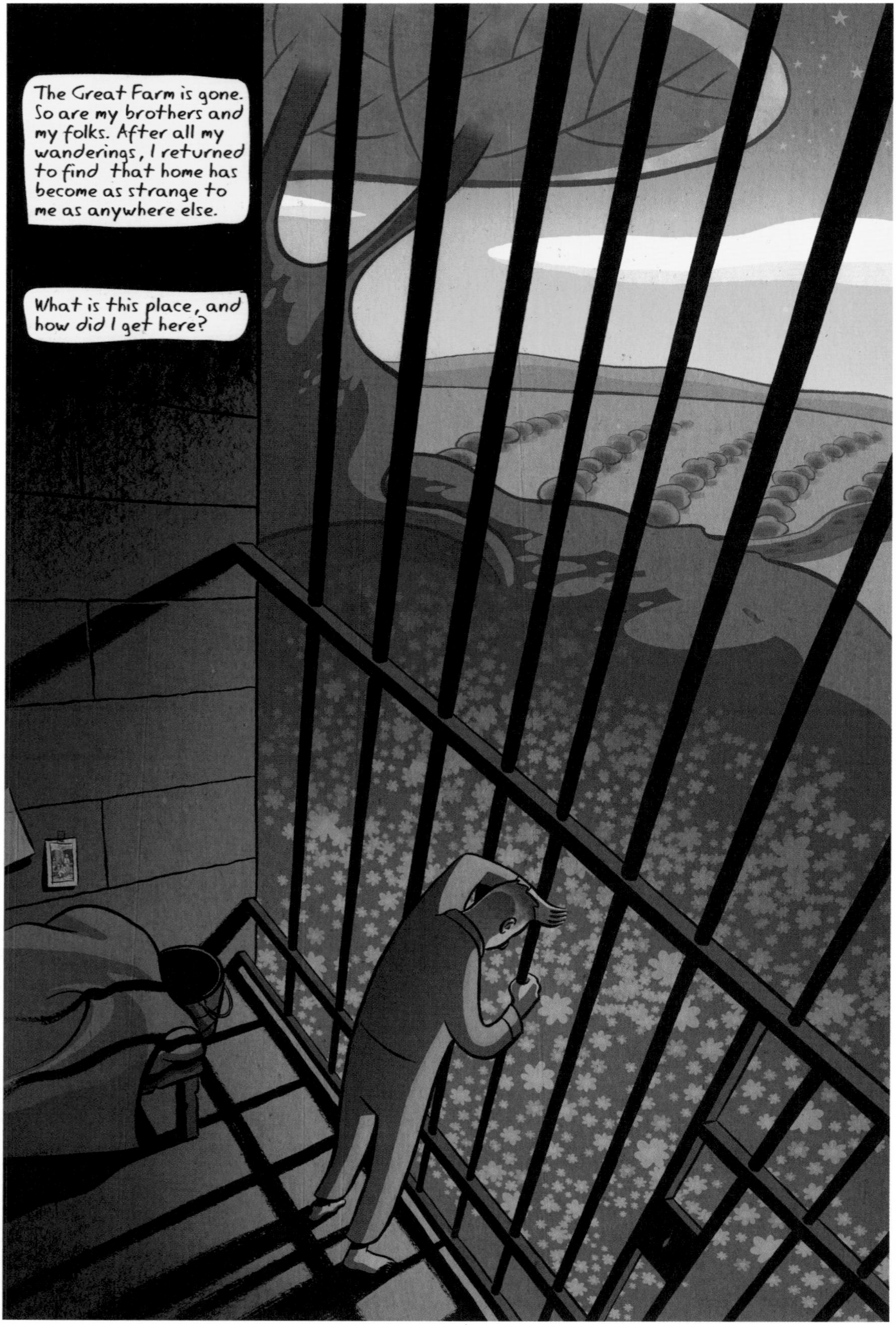
The Great Farm is gone. So are my brothers and my folks. After all my wanderings, I returned to find that home has become as strange to me as anywhere else.
What is this place, and how did I get here?

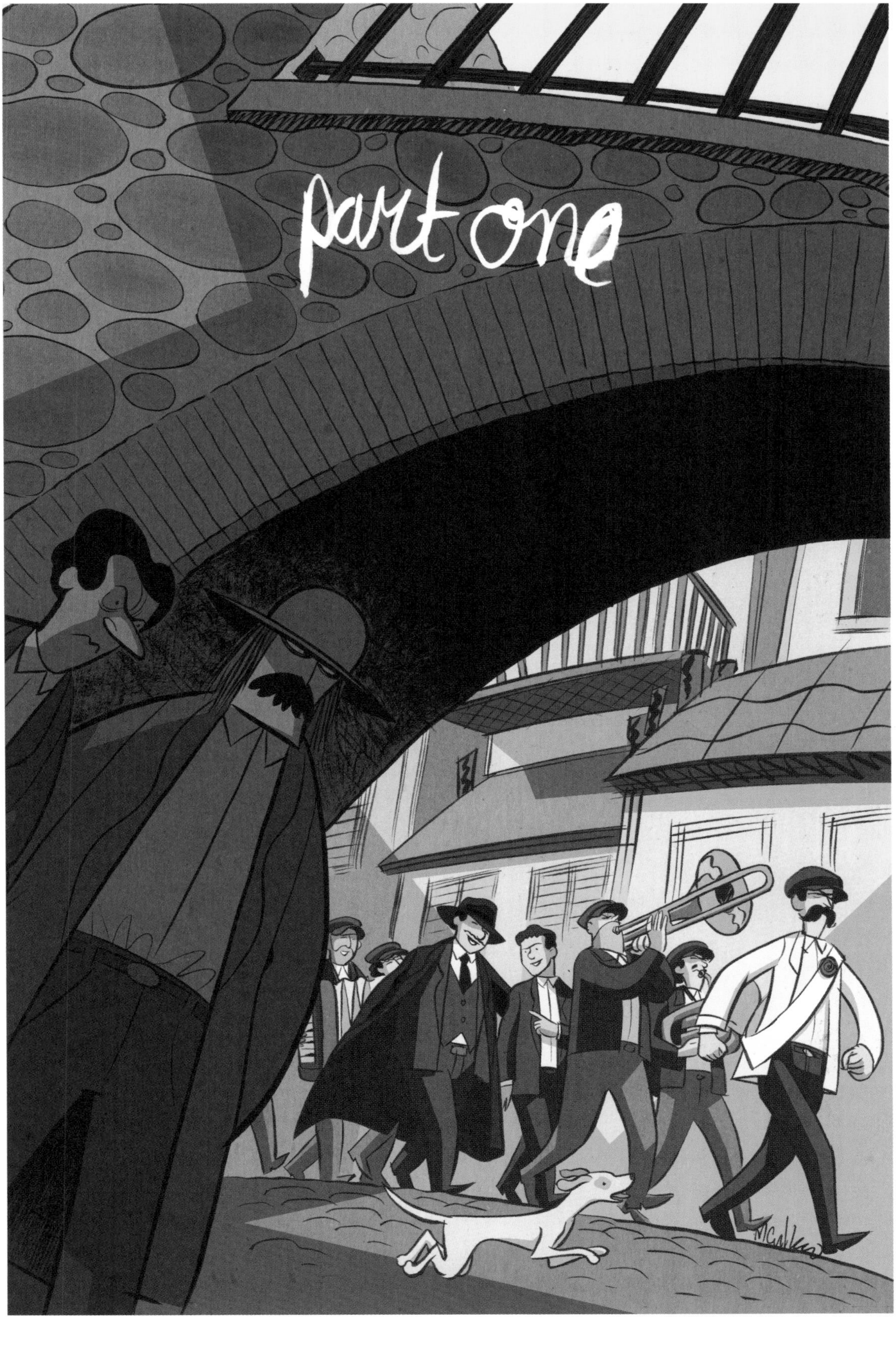
part one

PARTITO. SOCIALISTA
SEZIONE. DI.
It's great, Professor. My Mom's gonna love it.

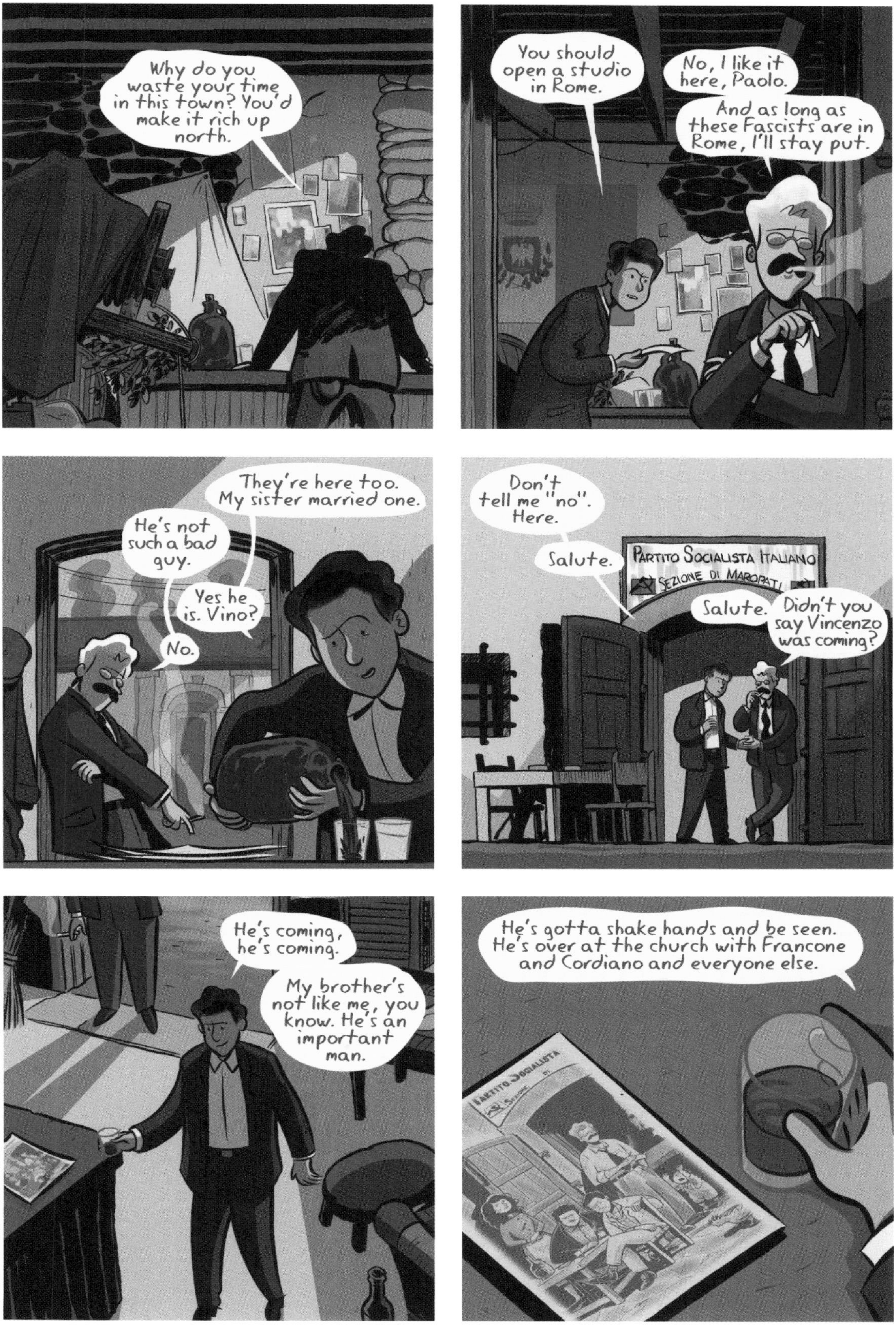
Why do you waste your time in this town? You'd make it rich up north.
You should open a studio in Rome.
No, I like it here, Paolo.
And as long as these Fascists are in Rome, I'll stay put.
They're here too. My sister married one.
He's not such a bad guy.
Yes he is. Vino?
No.
Don't tell me "no". Here.
Salute.
PARTITO SOCIALISTA ITALIANO
SEZIONE DI MAROPATI
Salute.
Didn't you say Vincenzo was coming?
He's coming, he's coming.
My brother's not like me, you know. He's an important man.
He's gotta shake hands and be seen. He's over at the church with Francone and Cordiano and everyone else.
PARTITO SOCIALISTA

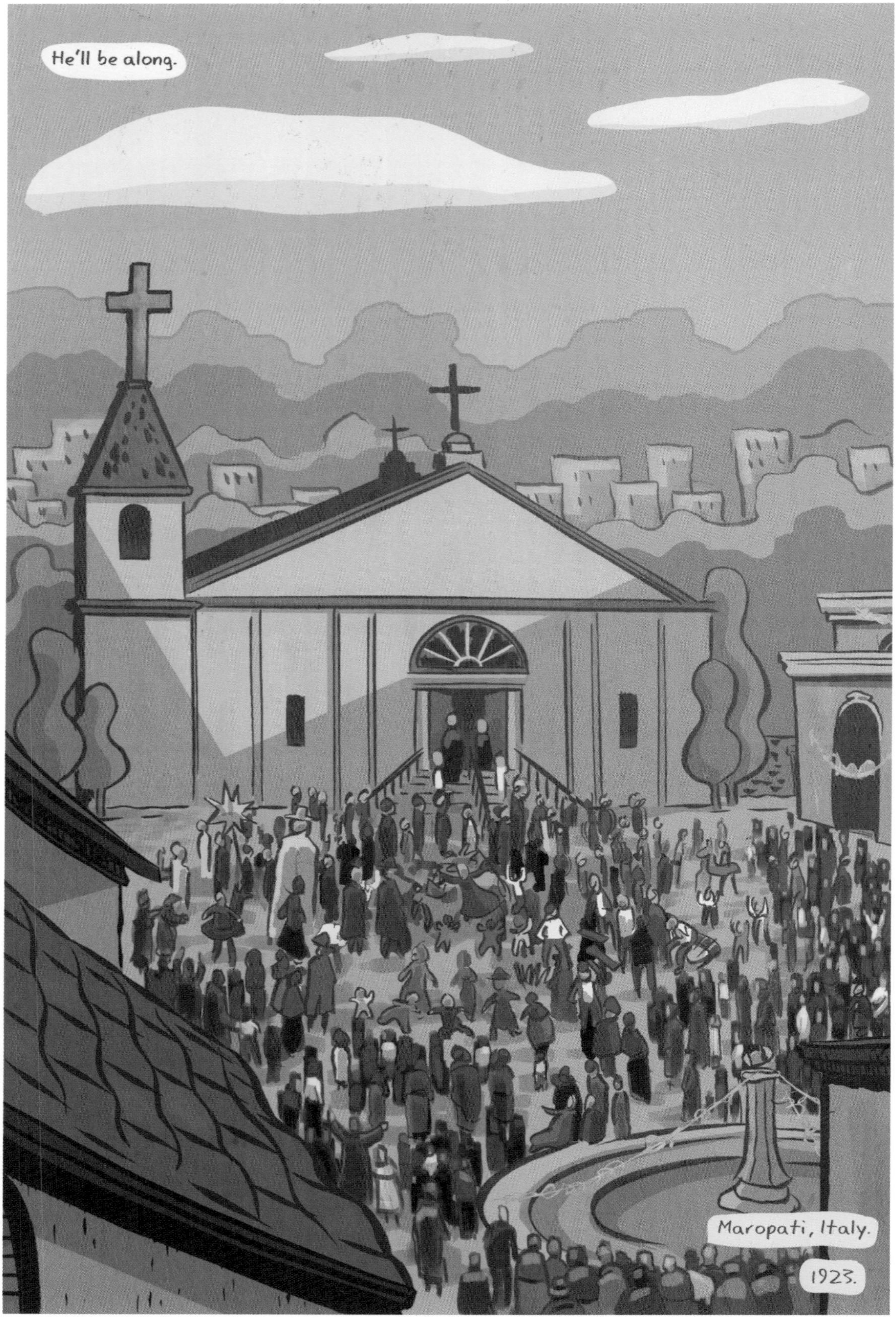
He'll be along.
Maropati, Italy.
1923.

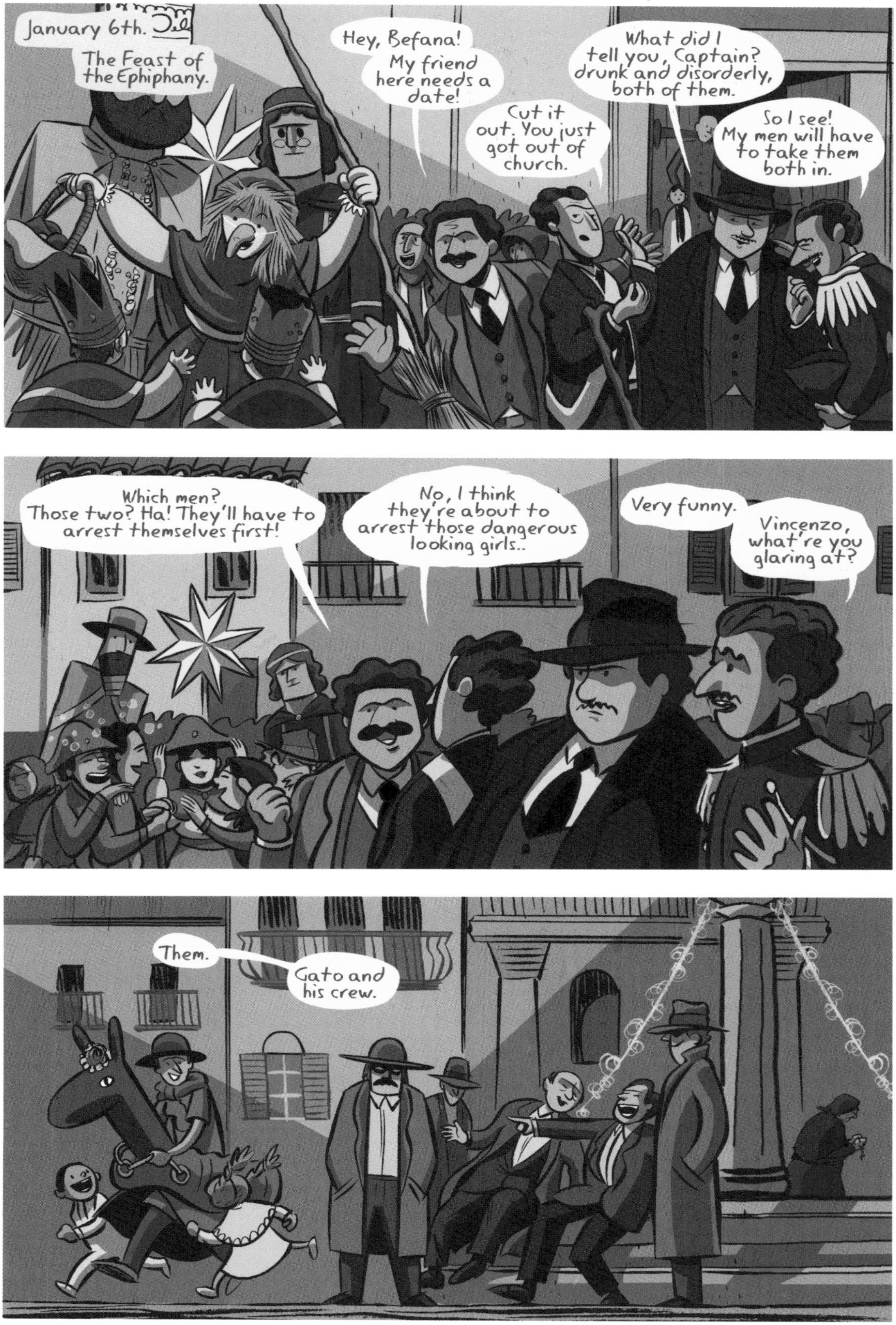
January 6th.
The Feast of the Ephiphany.
Hey, Befana!
My friend here needs a date!
Cut it out. You just got out of church.
What did I tell you, Captain? drunk and disorderly, both of them.
So I see! My men will have to take them both in.
Which men? Those two? Ha! They'll have to arrest themselves first!
No, I think they're about to arrest those dangerous looking girls..
Very funny.
Vincenzo, what're you glaring at?
Them.
Gato and his crew.

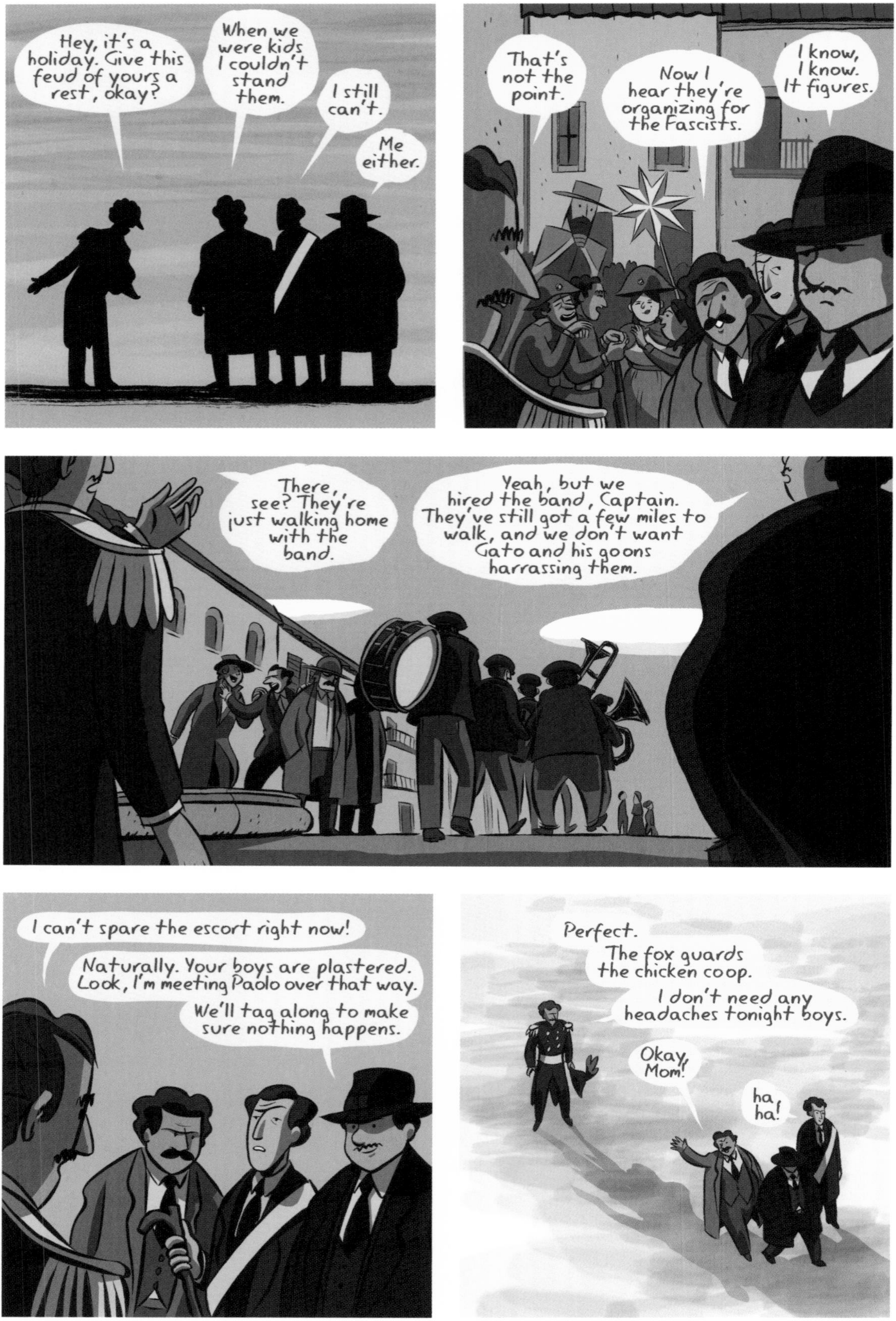
Hey, it's a holiday. Give this feud of yours a rest, okay?
When we were kids I couldn't stand them.
I still can't.
Me either.
That's not the point.
Now I hear they're organizing for the Fascists.
I know, I know. It figures.
There, see? They're just walking home with the band.
Yeah, but we hired the band, Captain. They've still got a few miles to walk, and we don't want Gato and his goons harrassing them.
I can't spare the escort right now!
Naturally. Your boys are plastered. Look, I'm meeting Paolo over that way.
We'll tag along to make sure nothing happens.
Perfect.
The fox guards the chicken coop.
I don't need any headaches tonight boys.
Okay, Mom!
ha ha!

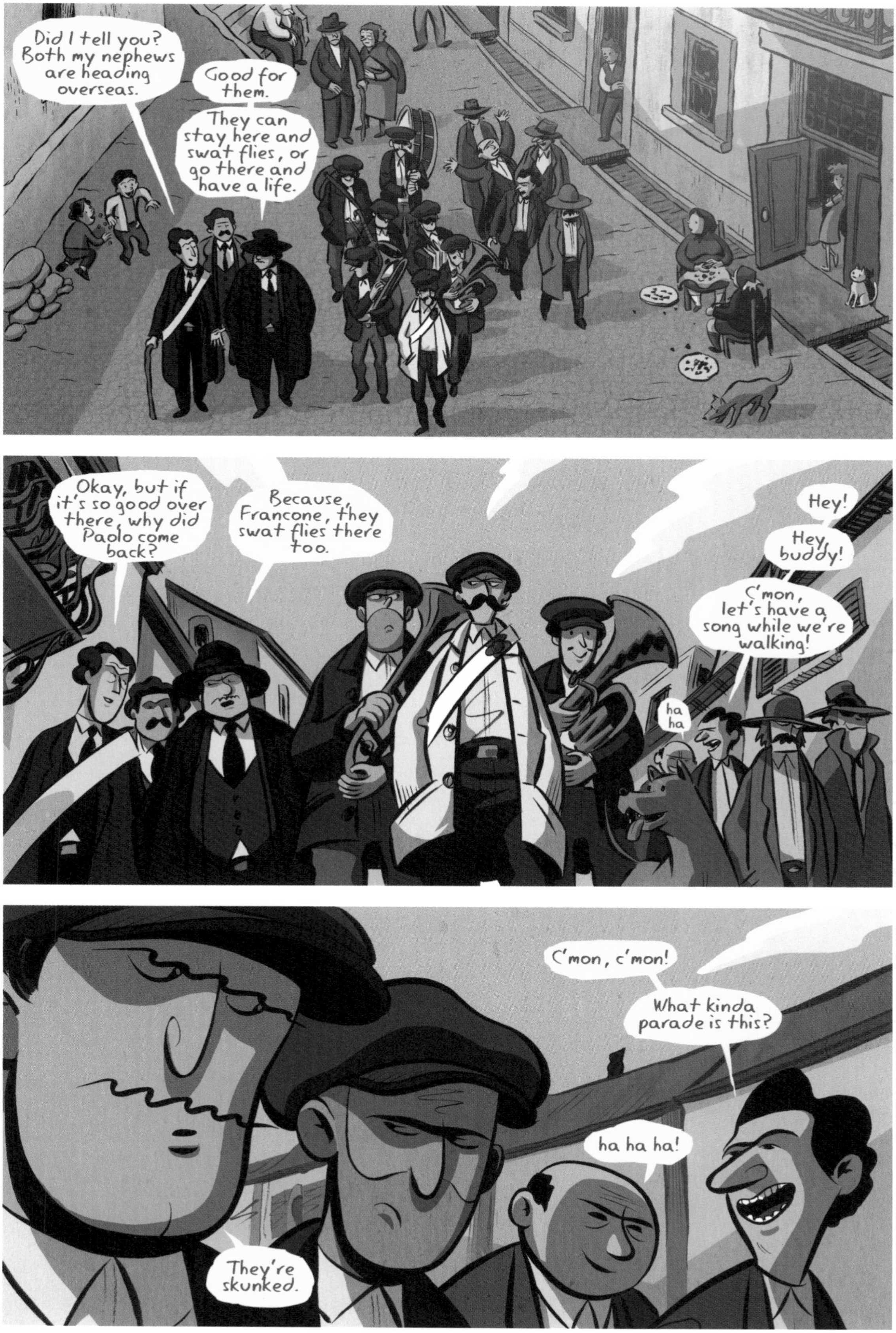
Did I tell you? Both my nephews are heading overseas.
Good for them.
They can stay here and swat flies, or go there and have a life.
Okay, but if it's so good over there, why did Paolo come back?
Because, Francone, they swat flies there too.
Hey!
Hey, buddy!
C'mon, let's have a song while we're walking!
ha ha
C'mon, c'mon!
What kinda parade is this?
ha ha ha!
They're skunked.

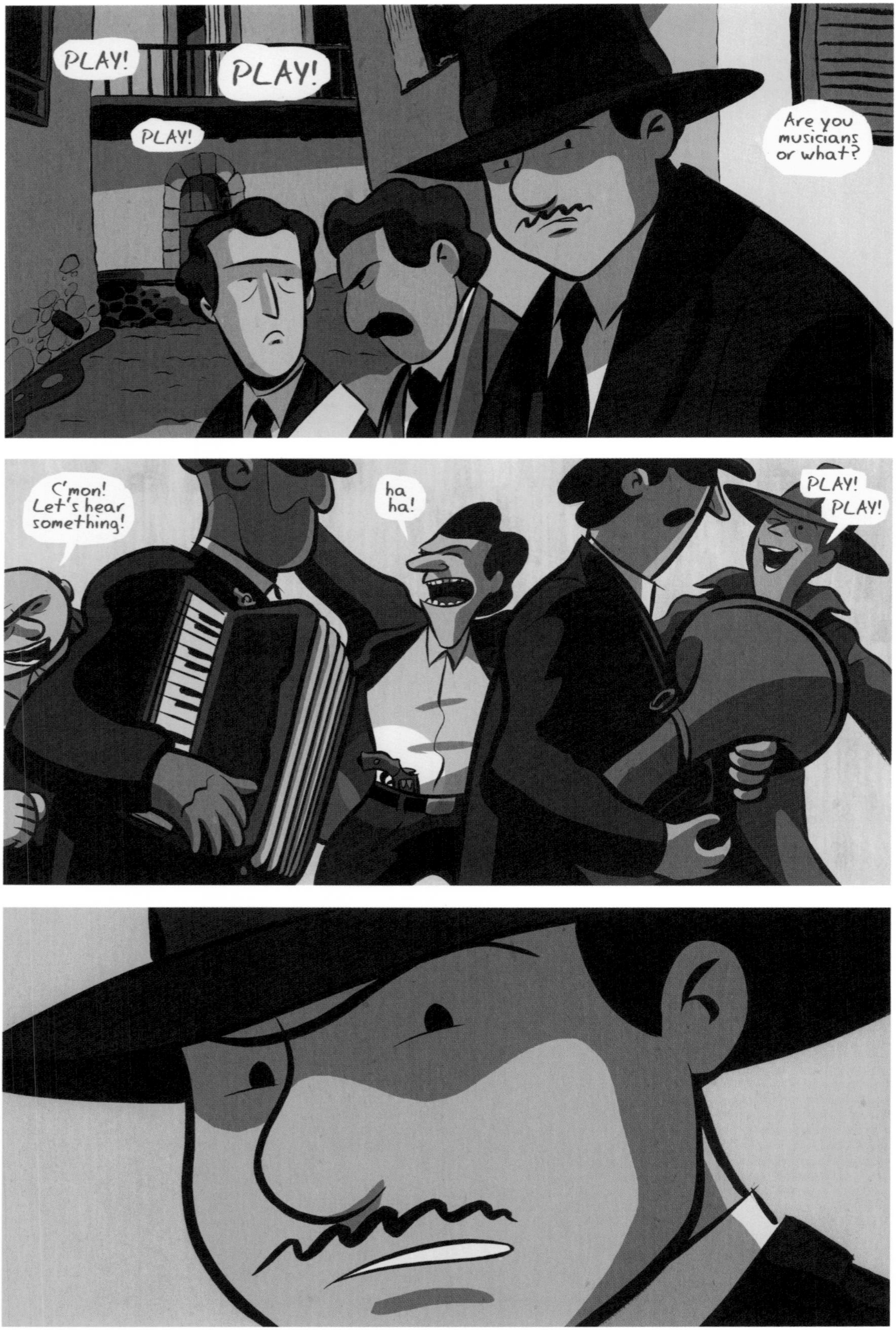
PLAY!
PLAY!
PLAY!
Are you musicians or what?
C'mon! Let's hear something!
ha ha!
PLAY! PLAY!

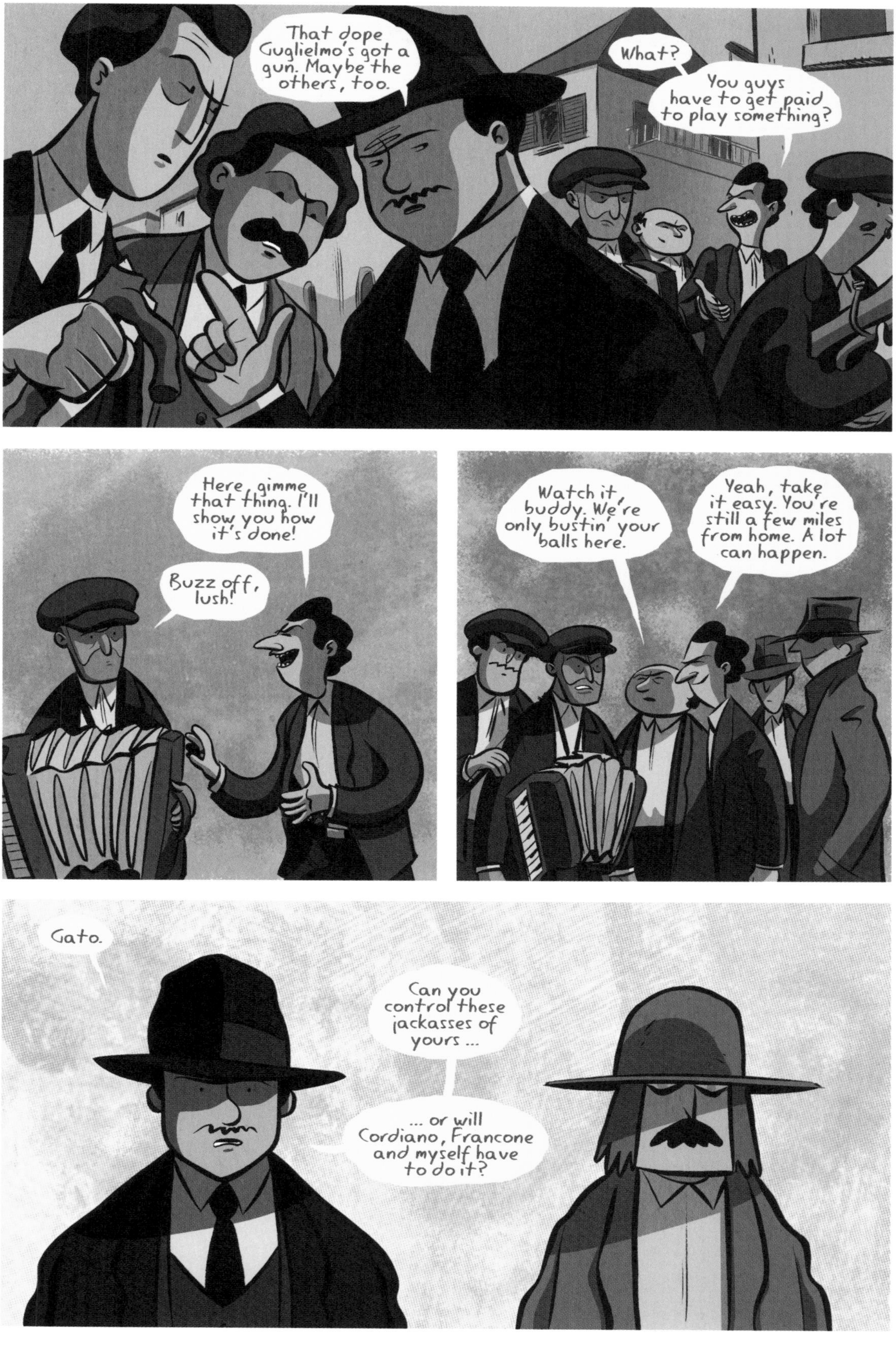
That dope Guglielmo's got a gun. Maybe the others, too.
What?
You guys have to get paid to play something?
Here, gimme that thing. I'll show you how it's done!
Buzz off, lush!
Watch it, buddy. We're only bustin' your balls here.
Yeah, take it easy. You're still a few miles from home. A lot can happen.
Gato.
Can you control these jackasses of yours ...
... or will Cordiano, Francone and myself have to do it?

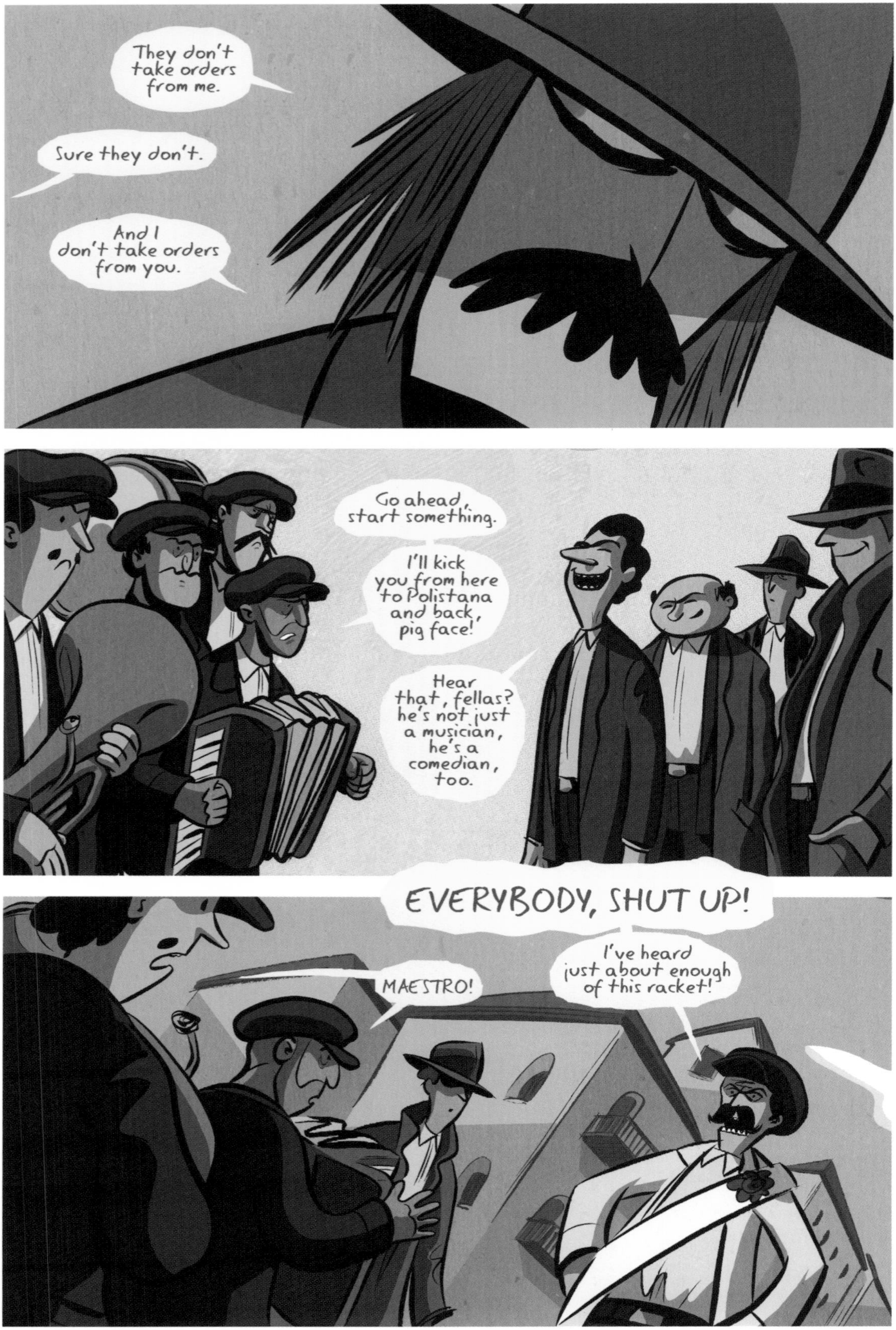
They don't take orders from me.
Sure they don't.
And I don't take orders from you.
Go ahead, start something.
I'll kick you from here to Polistana and back, pig face!
Hear that, fellas? he's not just a musician, he's a comedian, too.
EVERYBODY, SHUT UP!
MAESTRO!
I've heard just about enough of this racket!

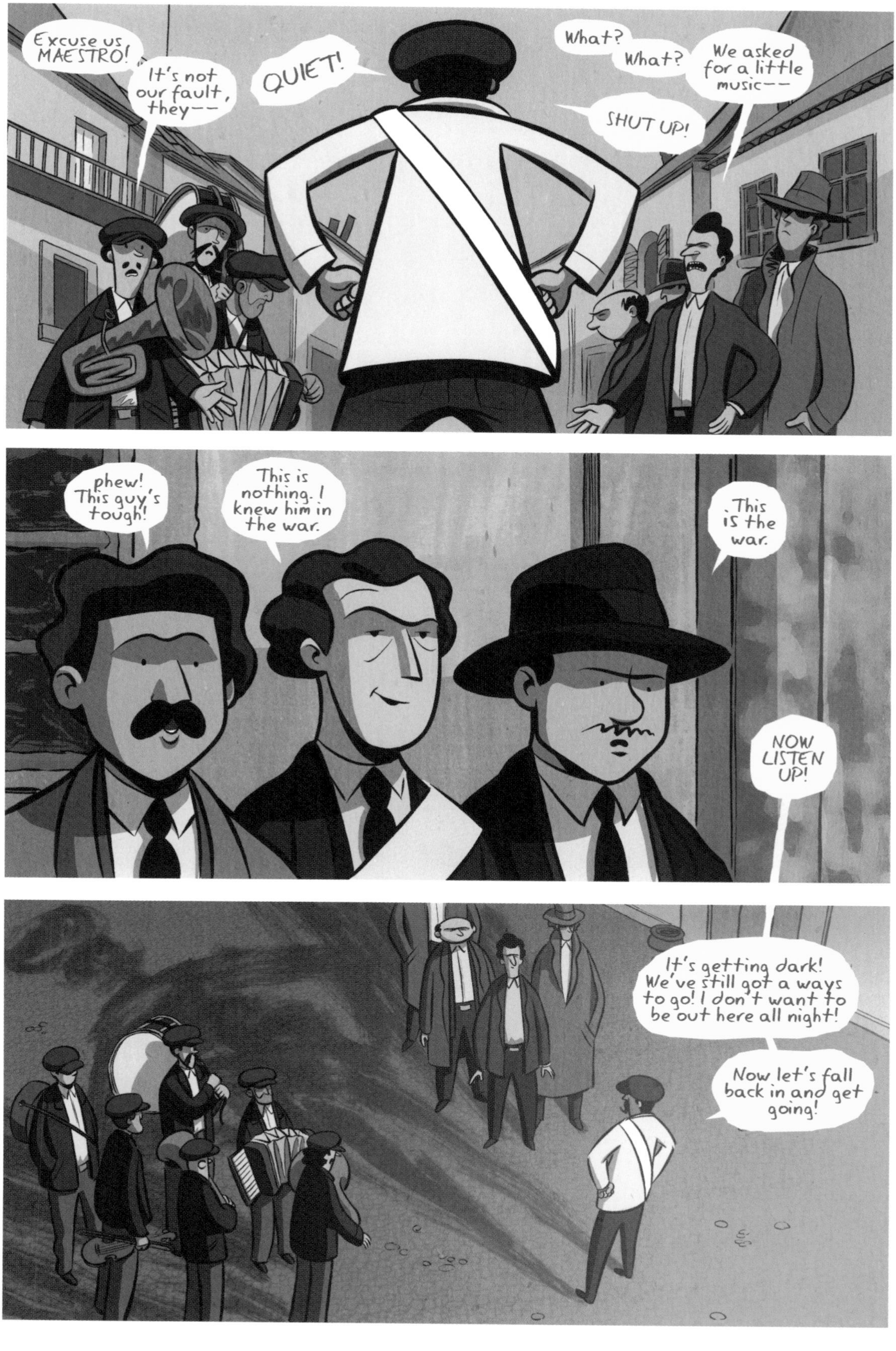
Excuse us MAESTRO!
It's not our fault, they--
QUIET!
What?
What?
We asked for a little music--
SHUT UP!
phew! This guy's tough!
This is nothing. I knew him in the war.
This is the war.
NOW LISTEN UP!
It's getting dark! We've still got a ways to go! I don't want to be out here all night!
Now let's fall back in and get going!

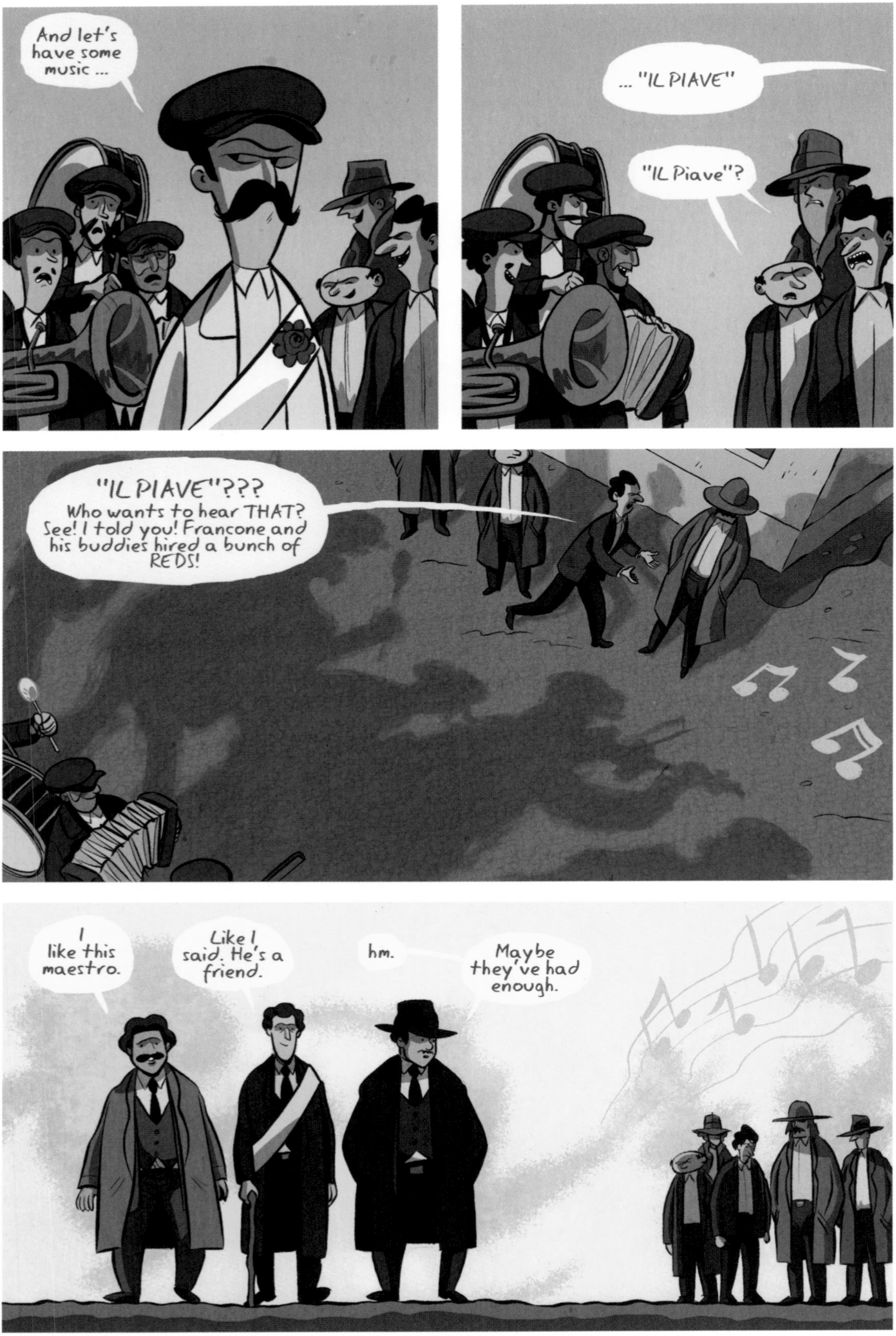
And let's have some music ...
... "IL PIAVE"
"IL Piave"?
"IL PIAVE"??? Who wants to hear THAT? See! I told you! Francone and his buddies hired a bunch of REDS!
I like this maestro.
Like I said. He's a friend.
hm.
Maybe they've had enough.

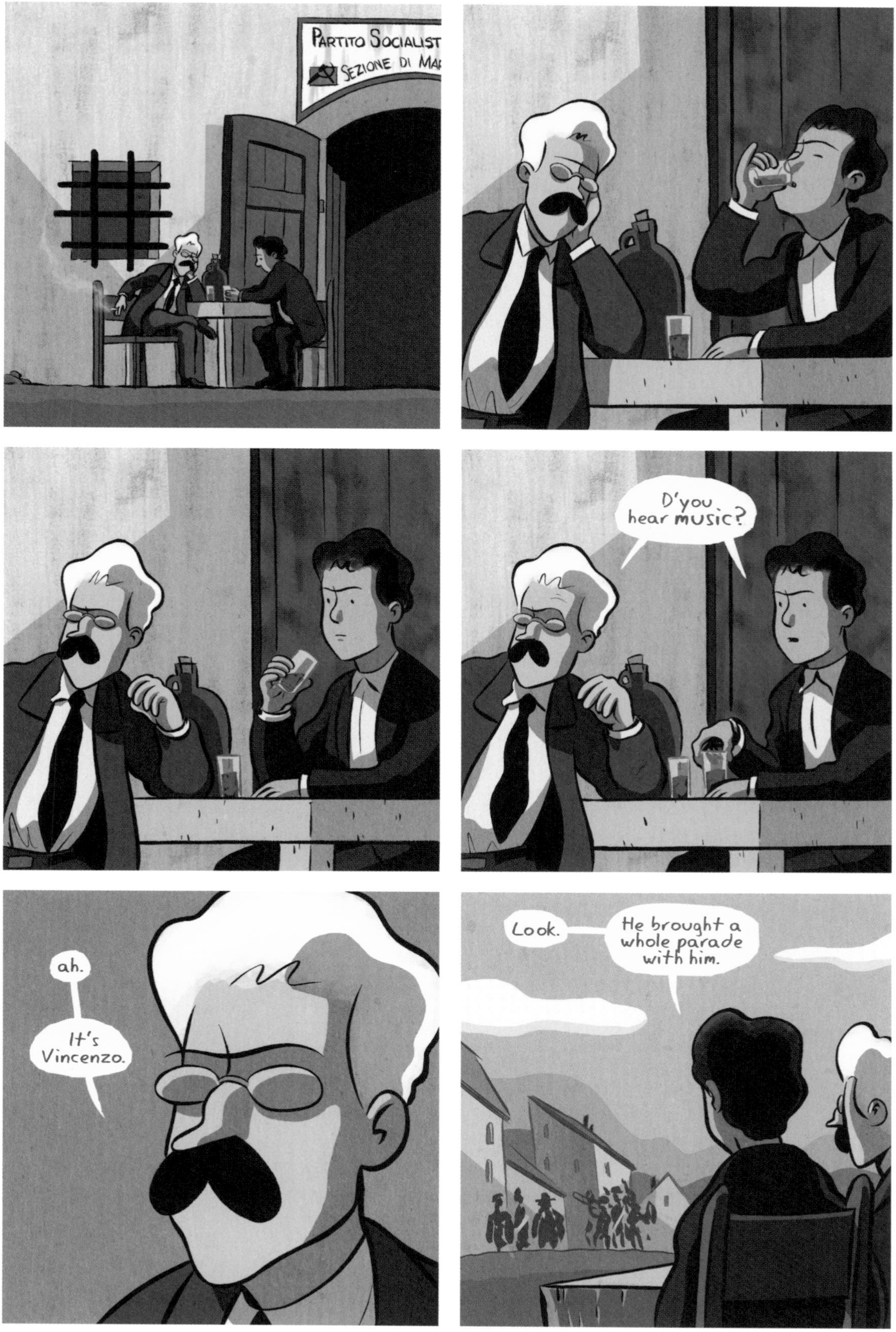
PARTITO SOCIALIST
SEZIONE DI MA
D'you hear music?
ah.
It's Vincenzo.
Look.
He brought a whole parade with him.

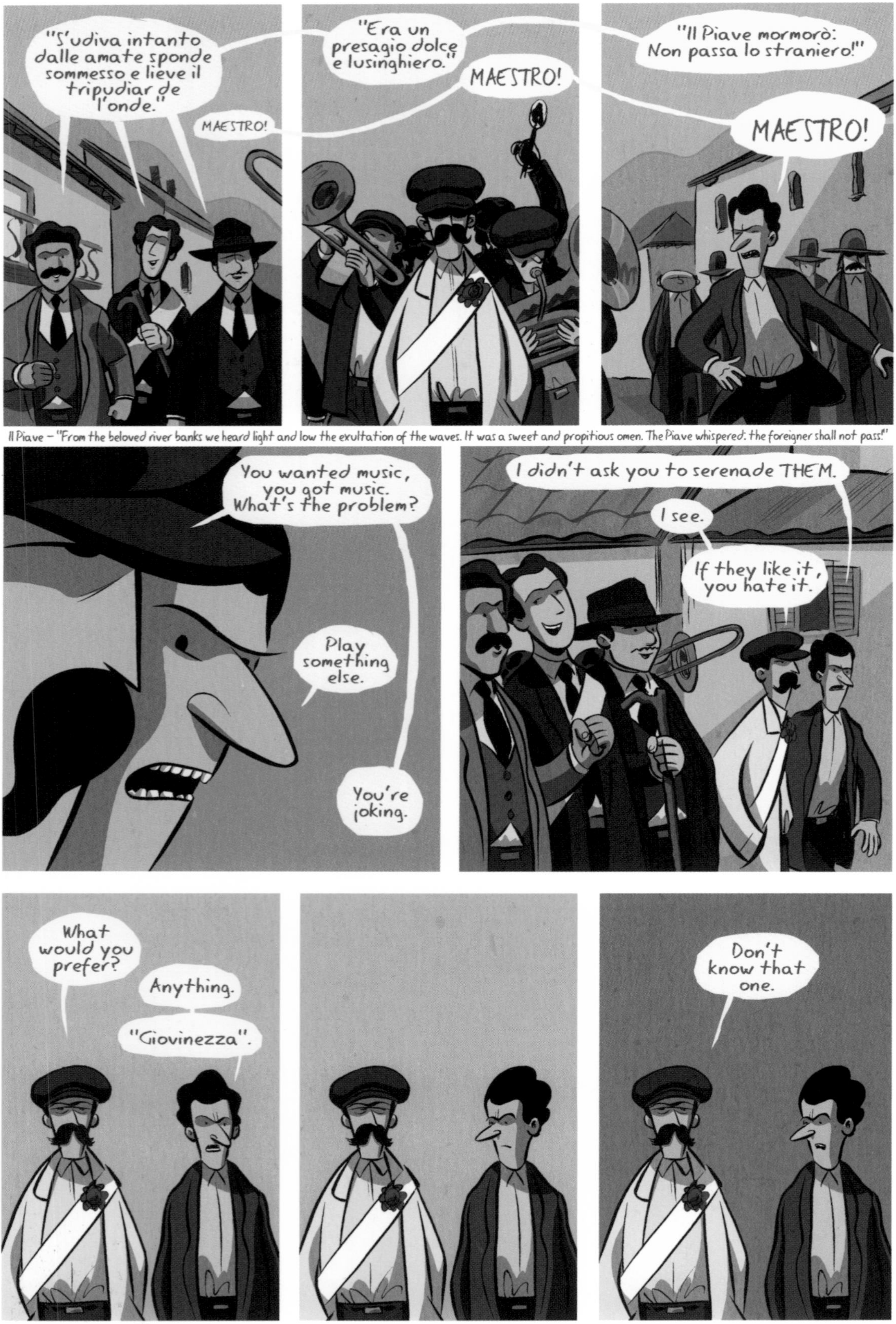
"S'udiva intanto dalle amate sponde sommesso e lieve il tripudiar de l'onde."
MAESTRO!
"Era un presagio dolce e lusinghiero."
MAESTRO!
"Il Piave mormorò: Non passa lo straniero!"
MAESTRO!
Il Piave – "From the beloved river banks we heard light and low the exultation of the waves. It was a sweet and propitious omen. The Piave whispered: the foreigner shall not pass!"
You wanted music, you got music. What's the problem?
Play something else.
You're joking.
I didn't ask you to serenade THEM.
I see.
If they like it, you hate it.
What would you prefer?
Anything.
"Giovinezza".
Don't know that one.

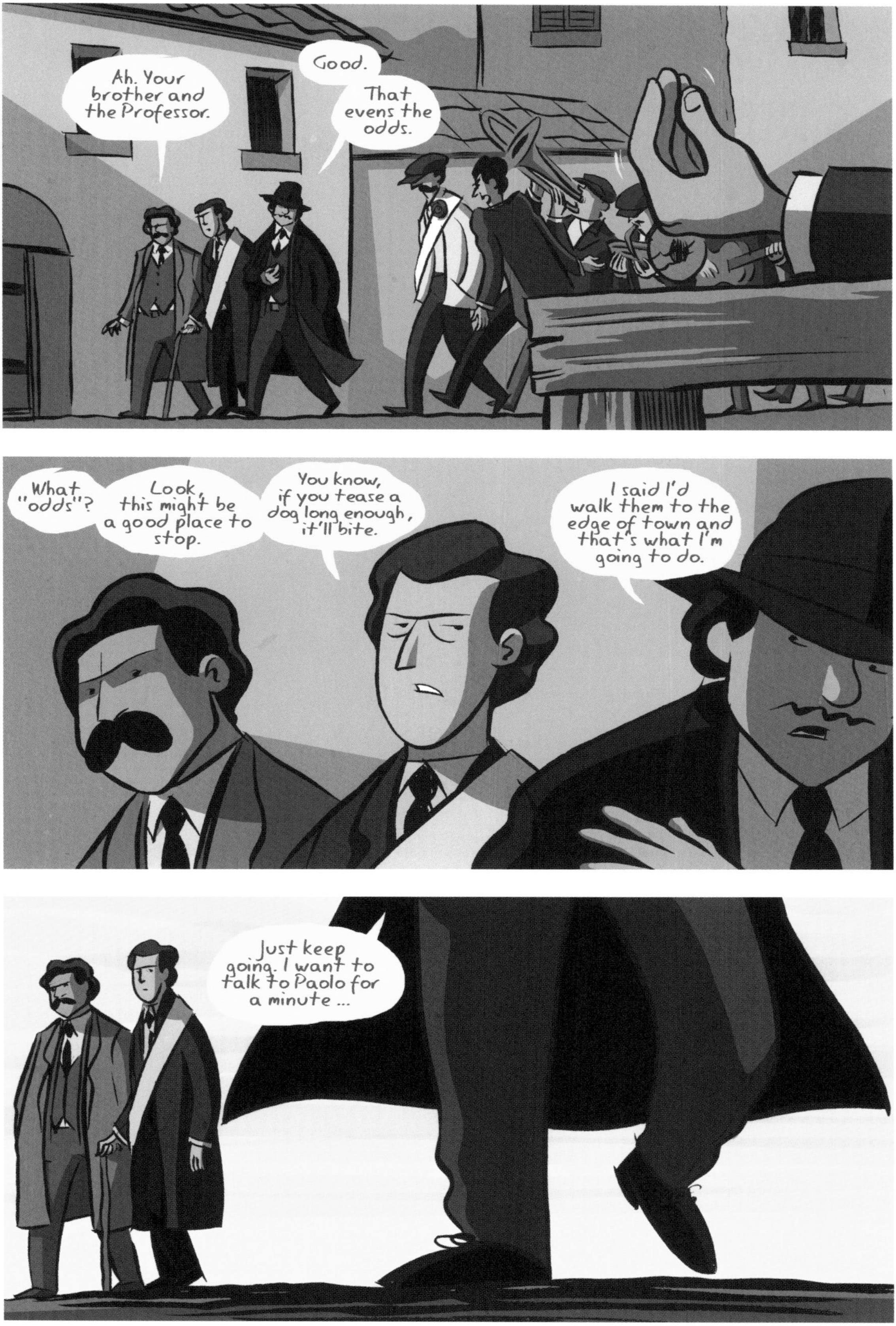
Ah. Your brother and the Professor.
Good.
That evens the odds.
What "odds"?
Look, this might be a good place to stop.
You know, if you tease a dog long enough, it'll bite.
I said I'd walk them to the edge of town and that's what I'm going to do.
Just keep going. I want to talk to Paolo for a minute ...

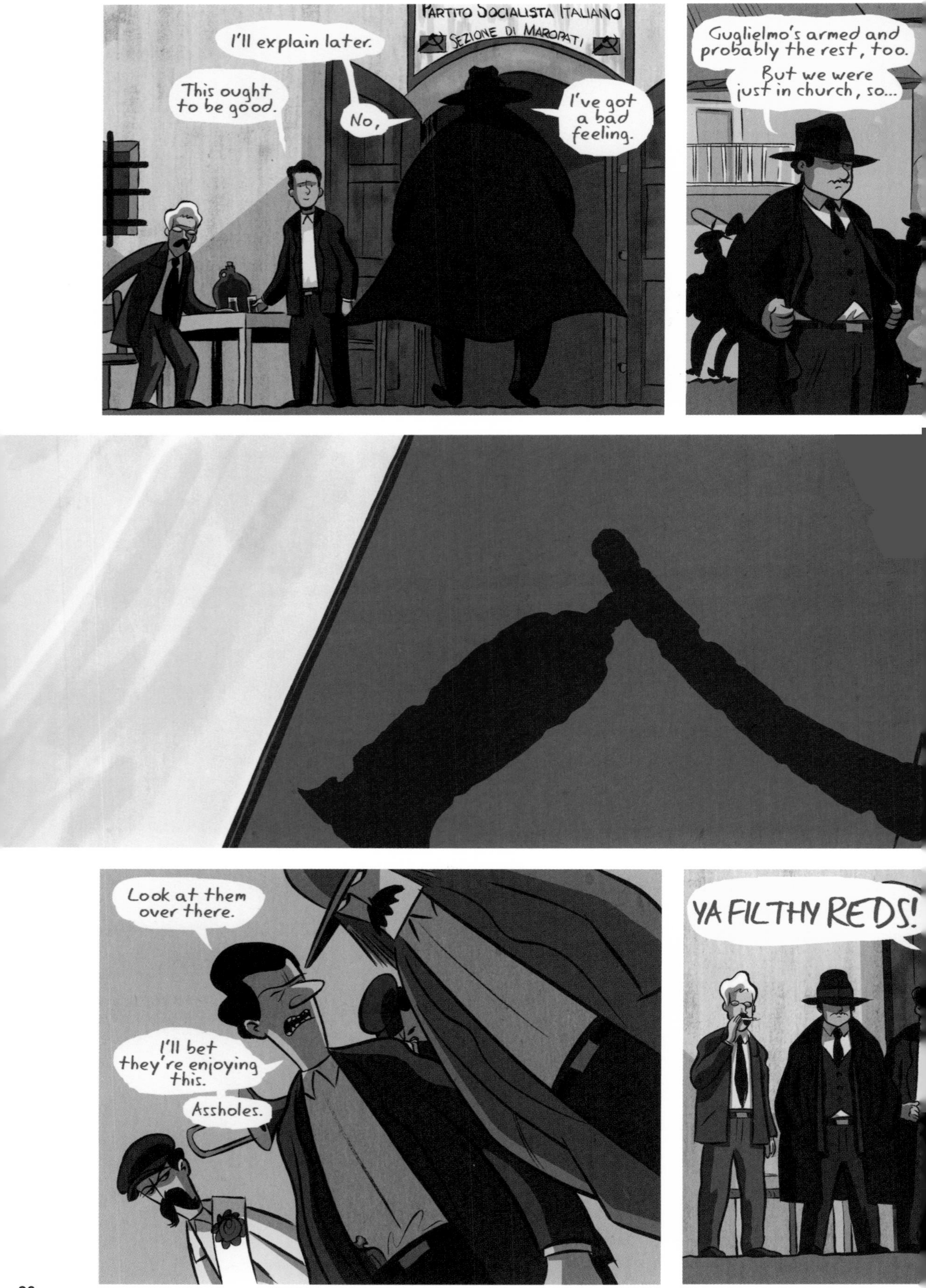
PARTITO SOCIALISTA ITALIANO
SEZIONE DI MAROPATI
I'll explain later.
This ought to be good.
No,
I've got a bad feeling.
Guglielmo's armed and probably the rest, too.
But we were just in church, so...
Look at them over there.
I'll bet they're enjoying this.
Assholes.
YA FILTHY REDS!

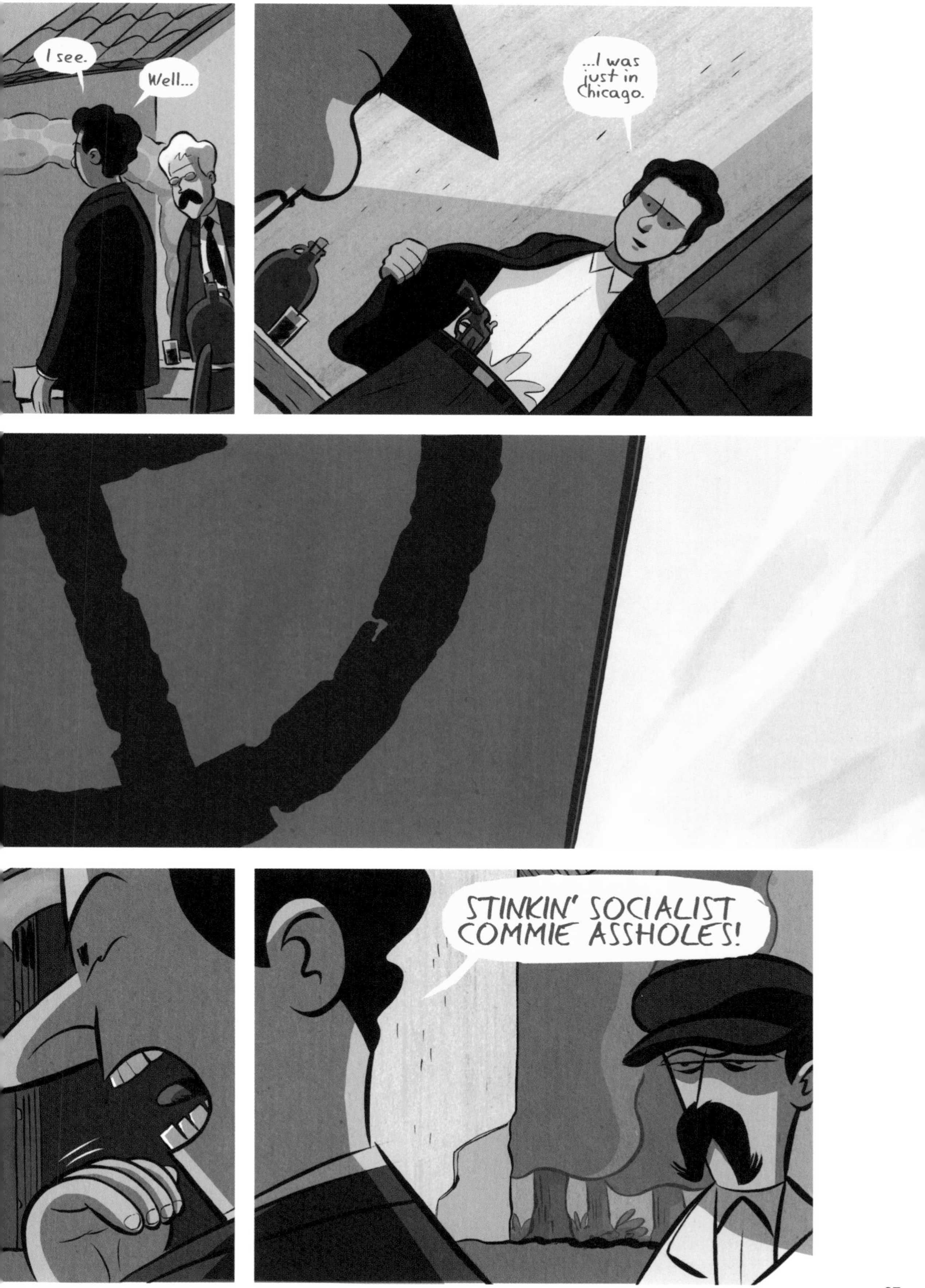
I see.
Well...
...I was just in Chicago.
STINKIN' SOCIALIST COMMIE ASSHOLES!

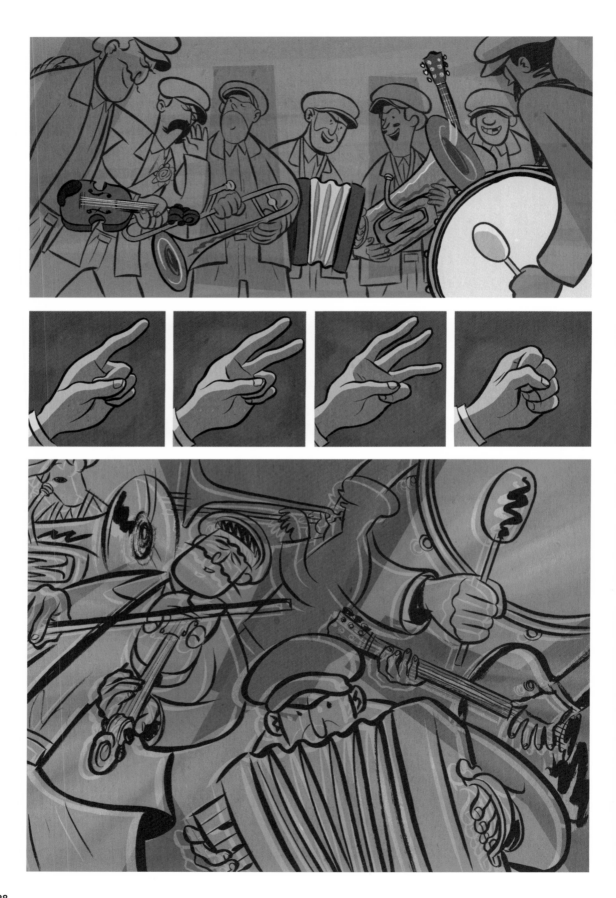

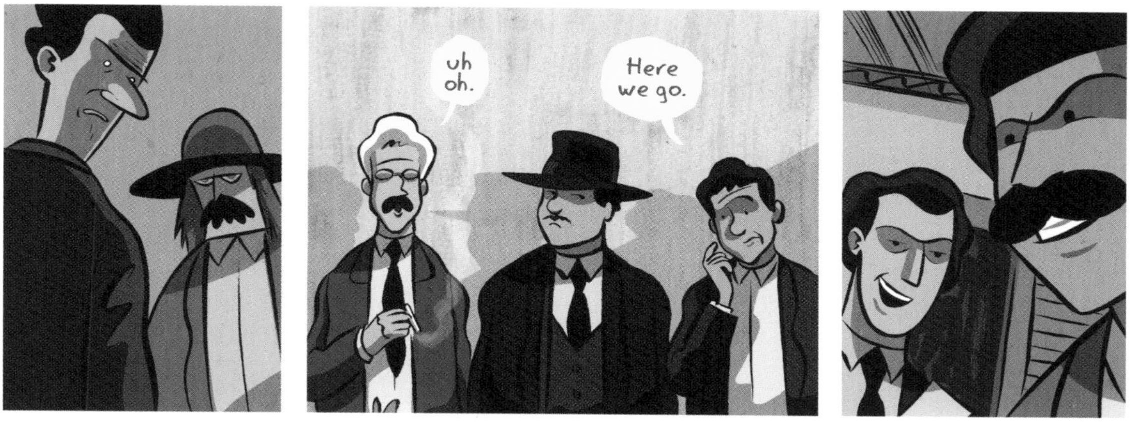

uh oh.
Here we go.

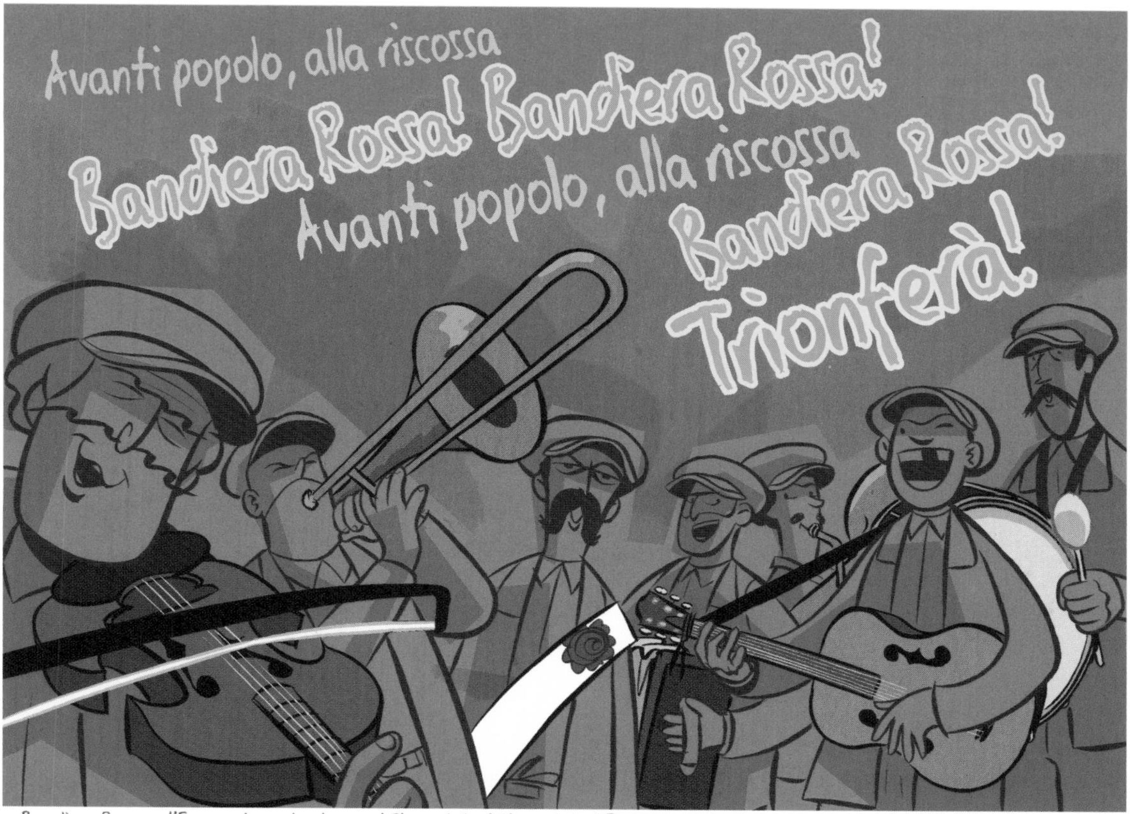

Avanti popolo, alla riscossa
Bandiera Rossa! Bandiera Rossa!
Avanti popolo, alla riscossa
Bandiera Rossa!
Trionferà!

Bandiera Rossa – "Forward people, to arms! The red flag! The red flag! Forward people, to arms! The red flag wll triumph!"

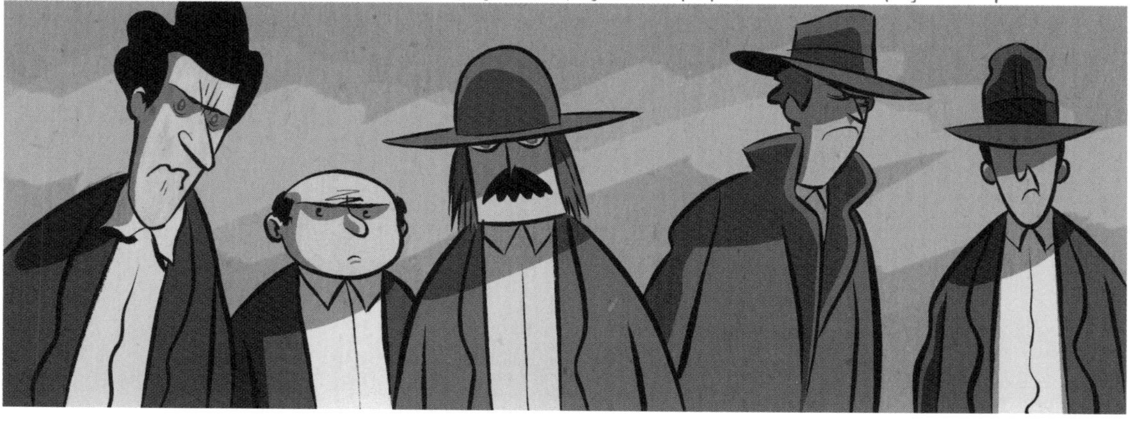

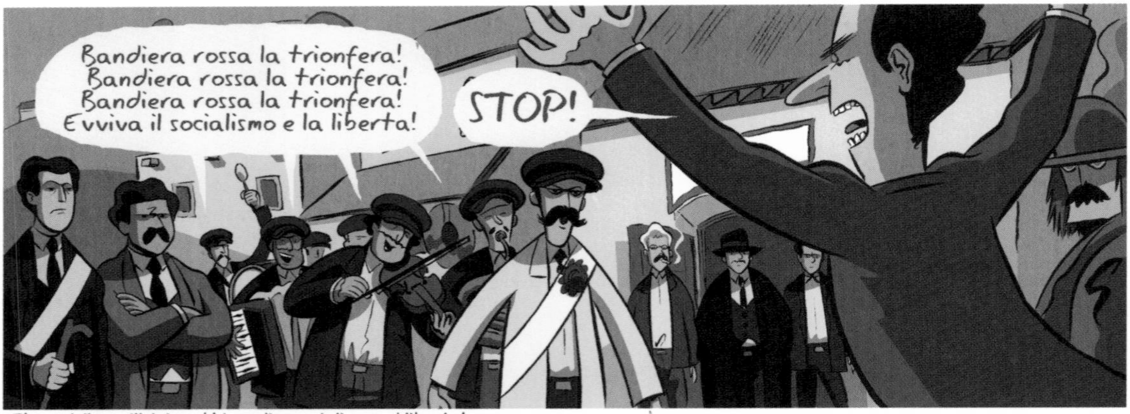
Bandiera rossa la trionfera!
Bandiera rossa la trionfera!
Bandiera rossa la trionfera!
Evviva il socialismo e la liberta!
STOP!

The red flag will triumph! Long live socialism and liberty!

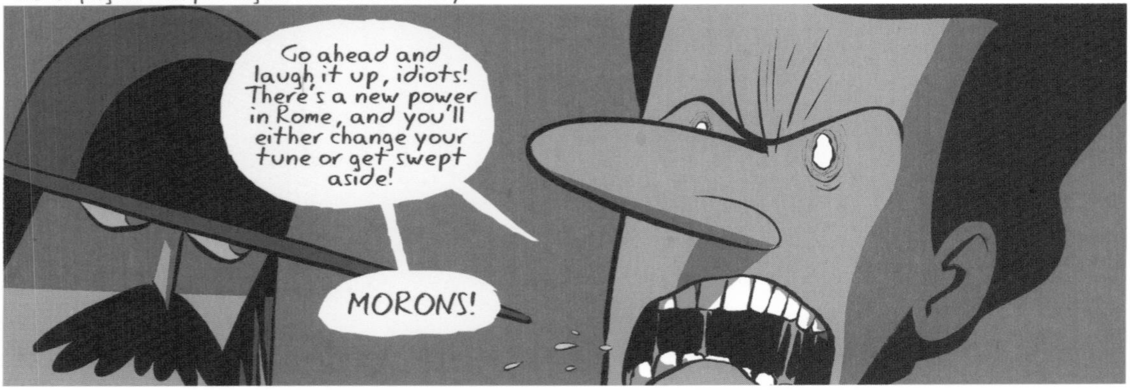
Go ahead and laugh it up, idiots! There's a new power in Rome, and you'll either change your tune or get swept aside!
MORONS!

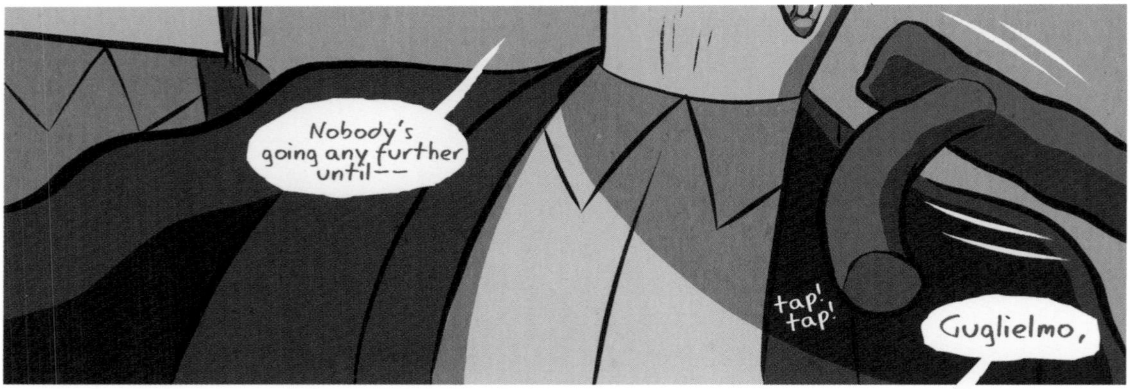
Nobody's going any further until--
tap! tap!
Guglielmo,

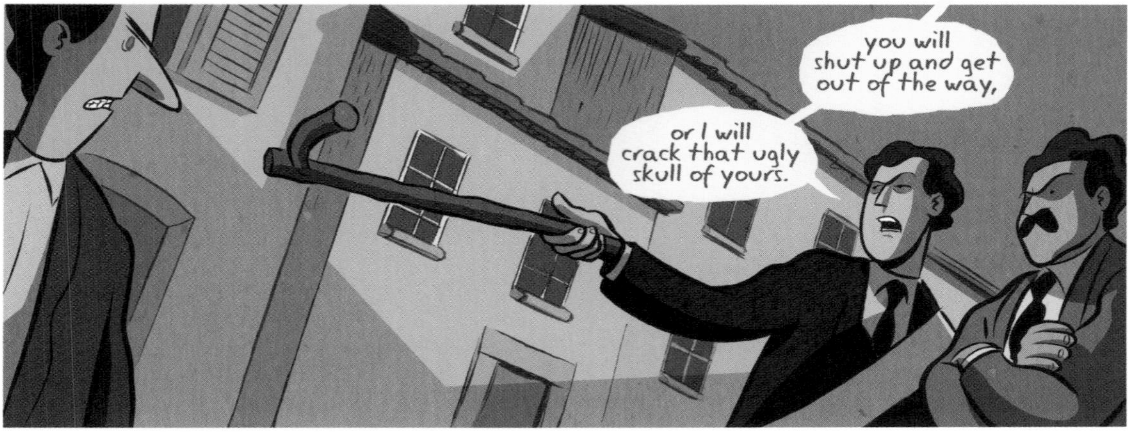
you will shut up and get out of the way,
or I will crack that ugly skull of yours.

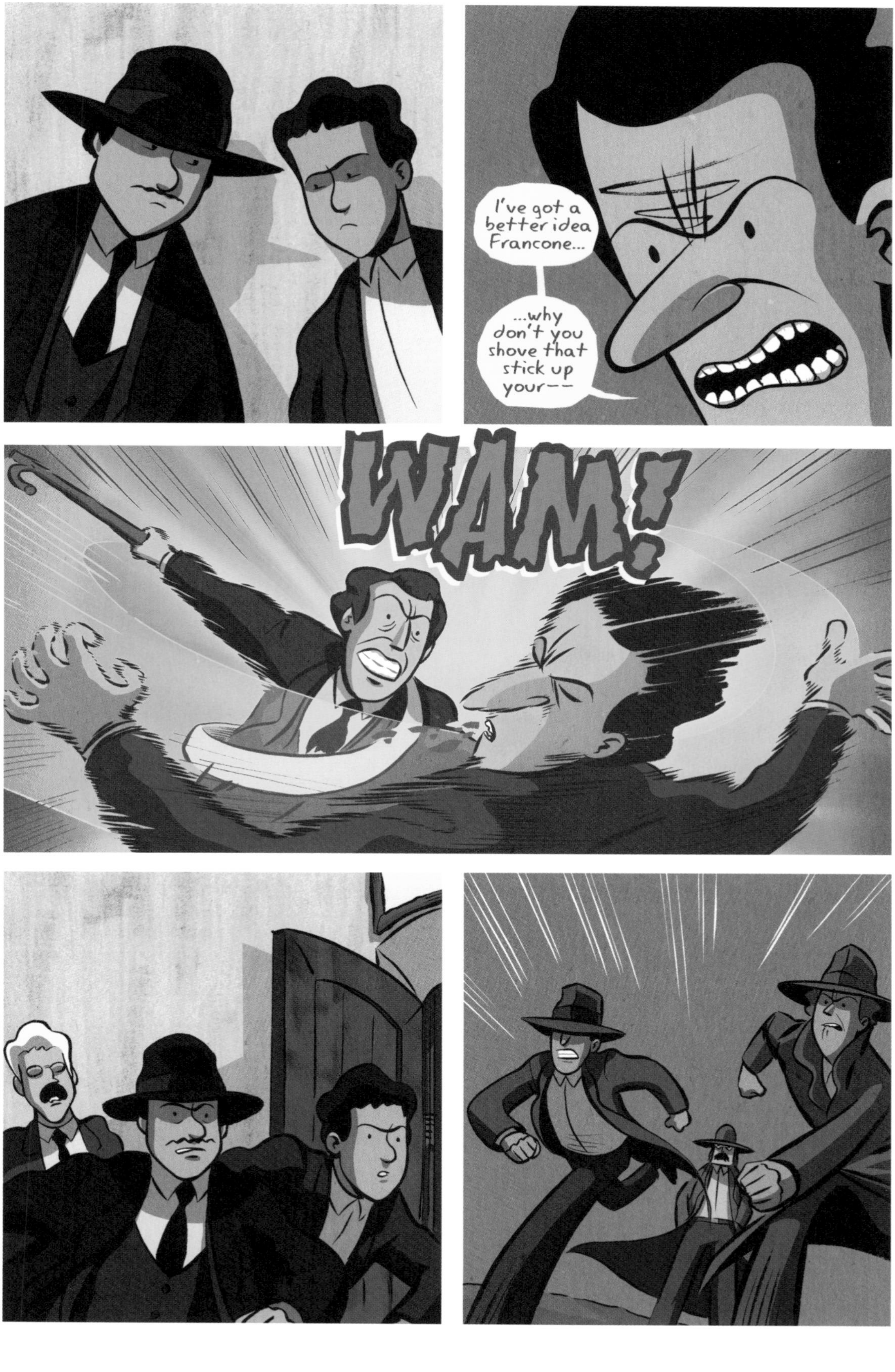
I've got a better idea Francone...
...why don't you shove that stick up your--
WAM!

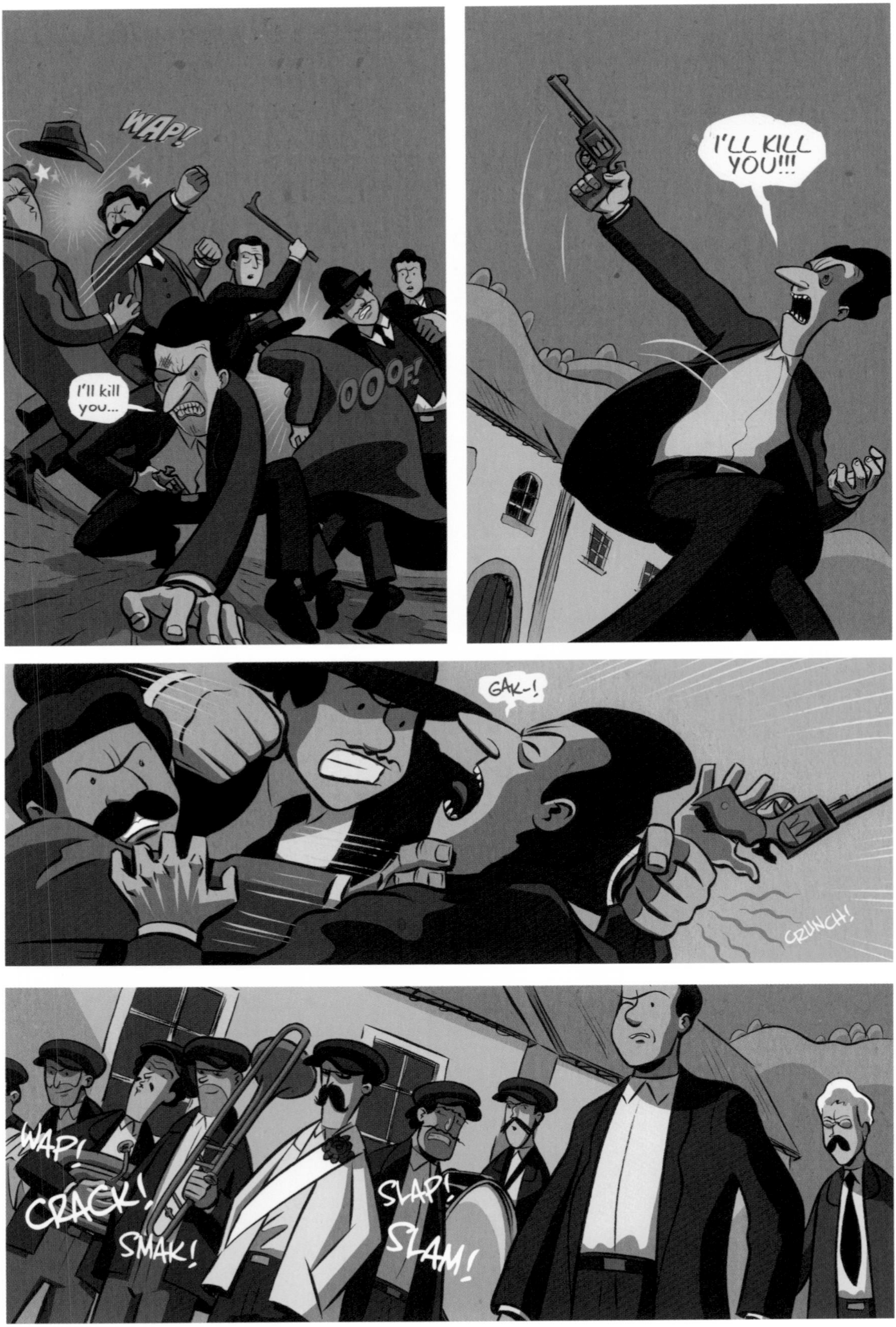
WAP!
I'll kill you...
OOOF!
I'LL KILL YOU!!!
GAK-!
CRUNCH!
WAP!
CRACK!
SMAK!
SLAP!
SLAM!

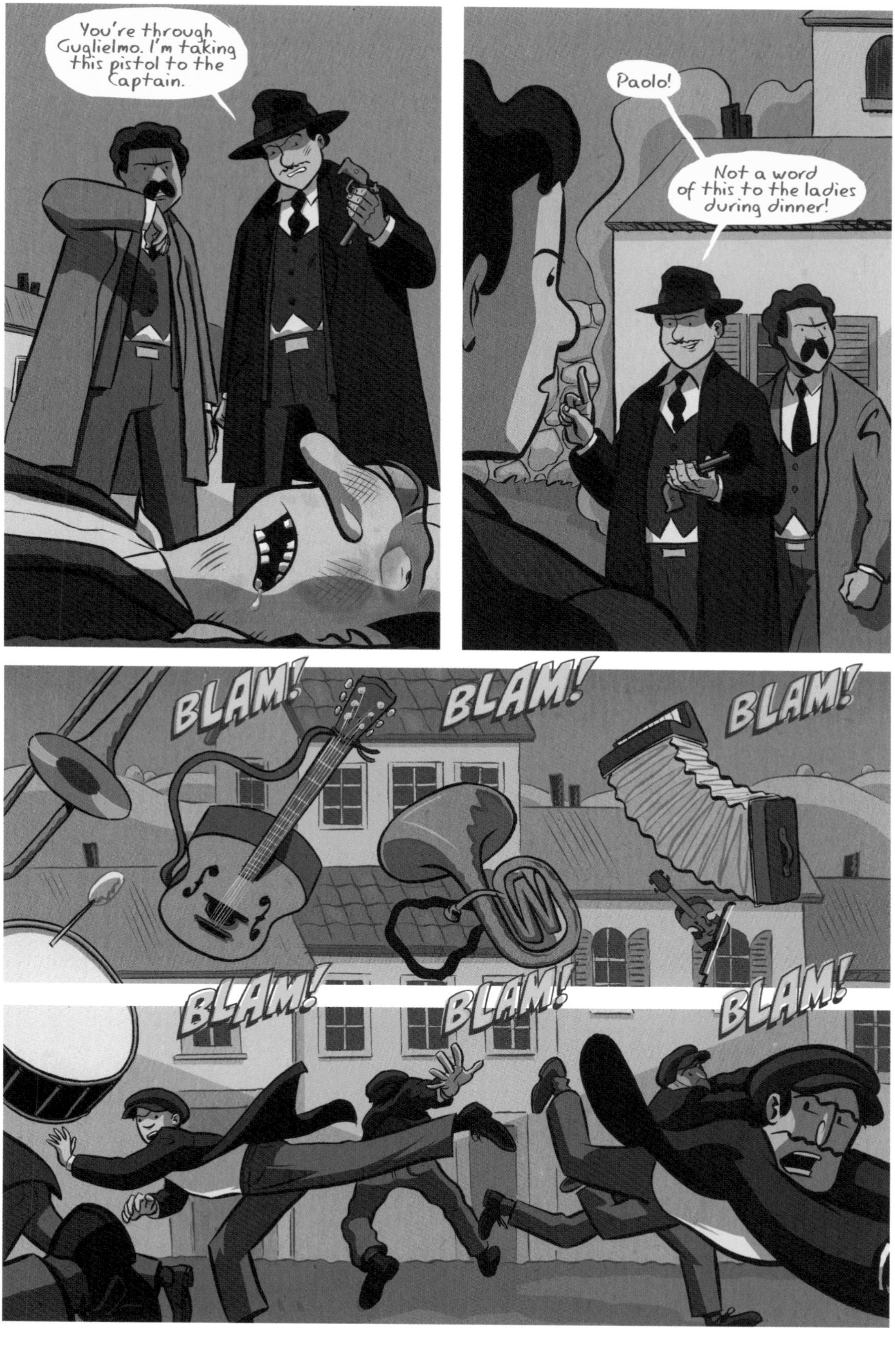
You're through Guglielmo. I'm taking this pistol to the Captain.
Paolo!
Not a word of this to the ladies during dinner!
BLAM!
BLAM!
BLAM!
BLAM!
BLAM!
BLAM!

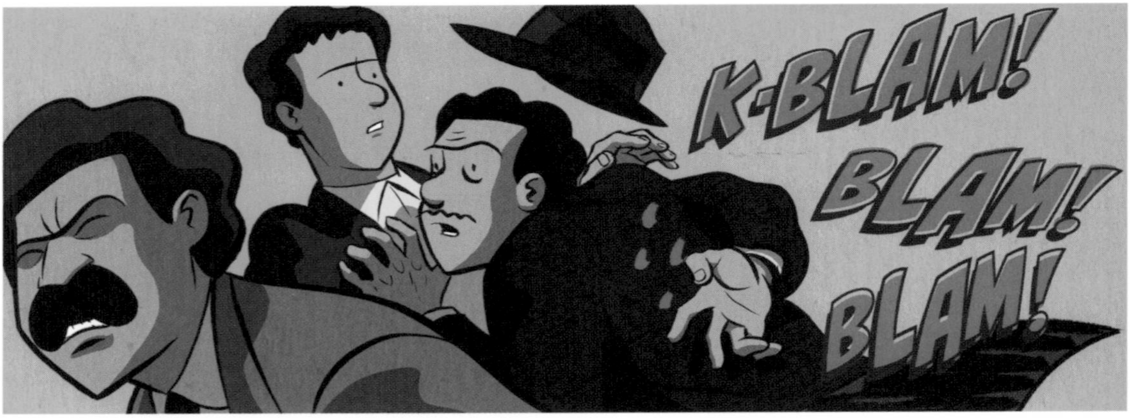
K-BLAM!
BLAM!
BLAM!

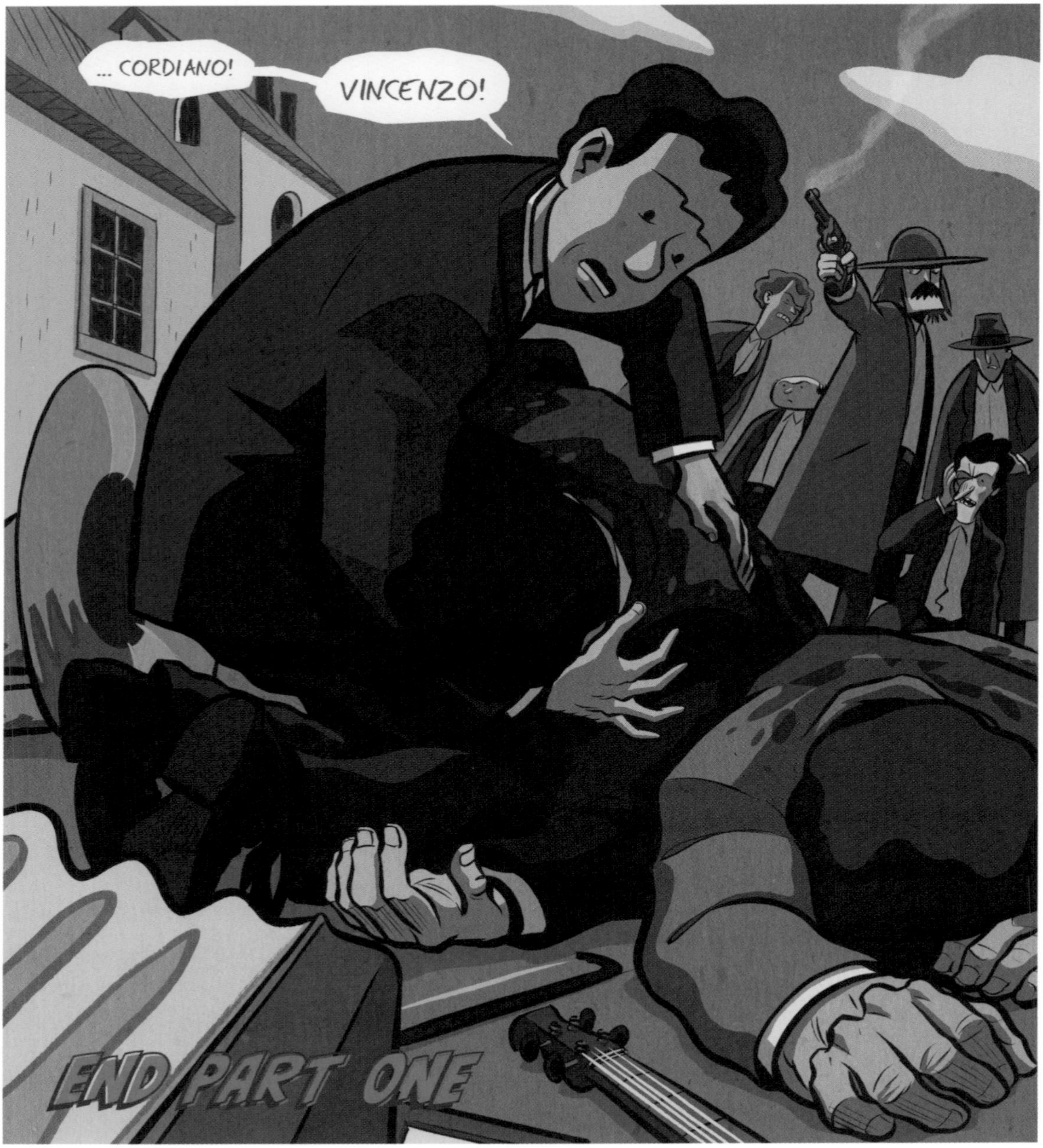
... CORDIANO!
VINCENZO!
END PART ONE

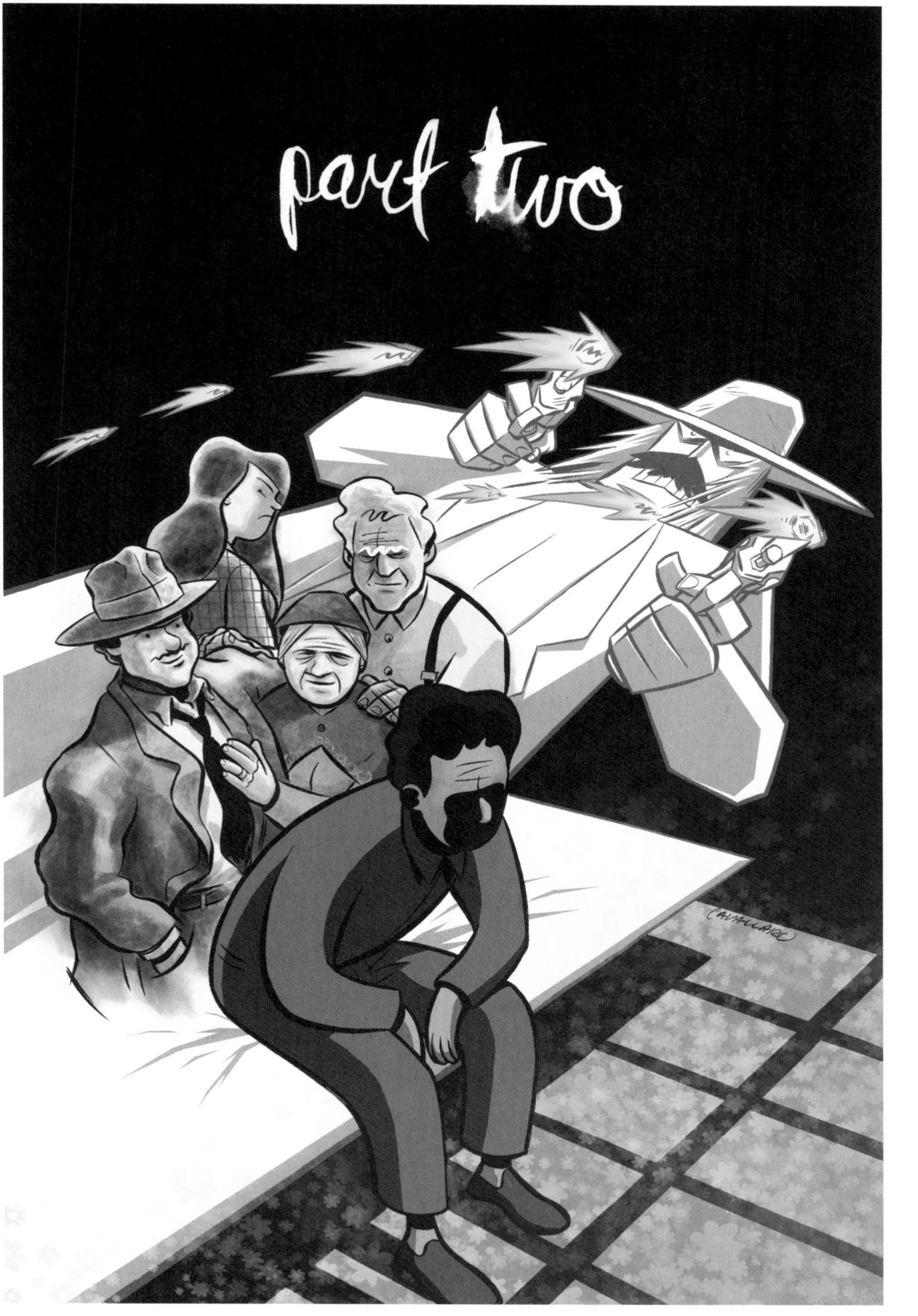
part two
CAVALLARO

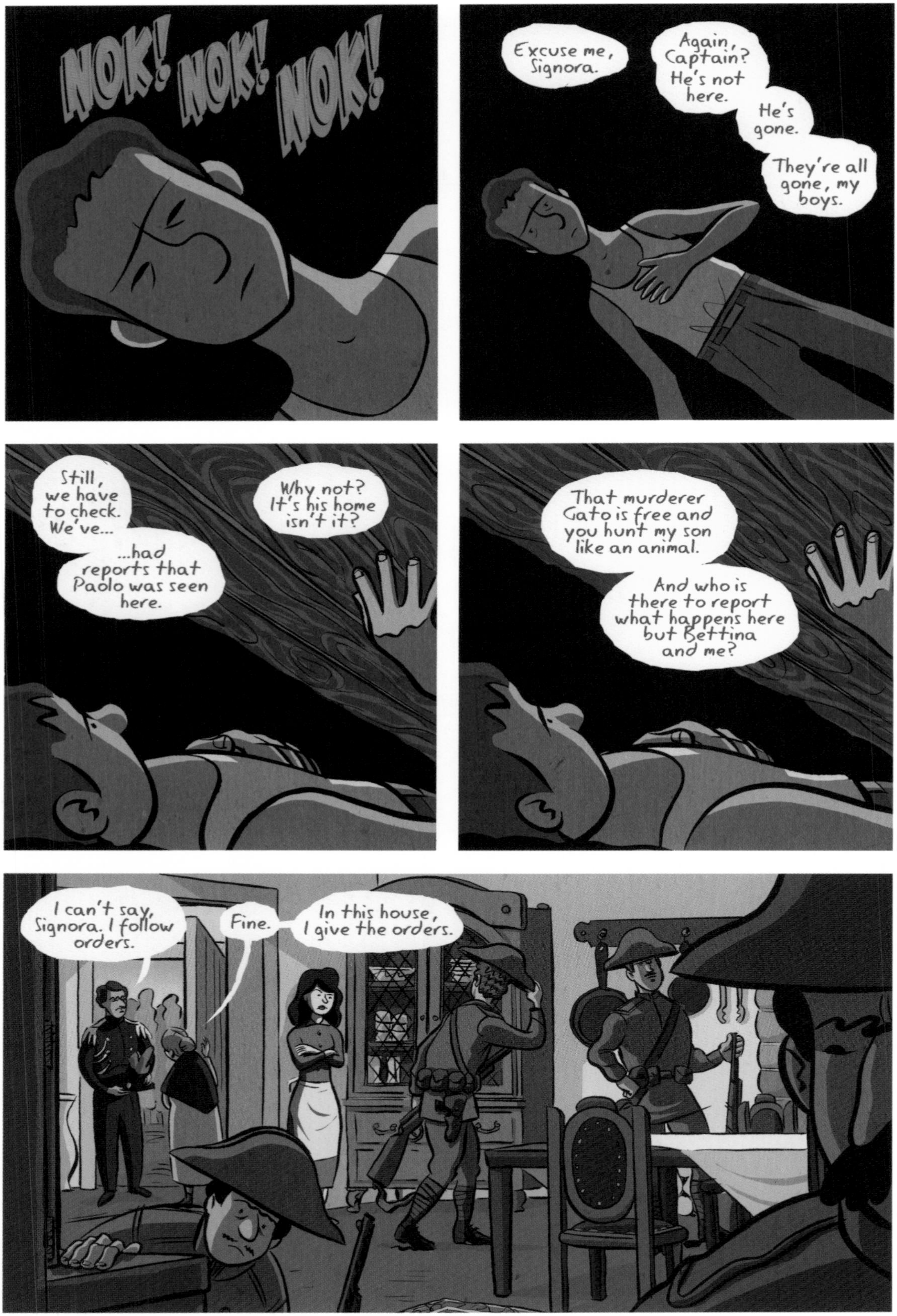
NOK! NOK! NOK!
Excuse me, Signora.
Again, Captain? He's not here.
He's gone.
They're all gone, my boys.
Still, we have to check. We've...
...had reports that Paolo was seen here.
Why not? It's his home isn't it?
That murderer Gato is free and you hunt my son like an animal.
And who is there to report what happens here but Bettina and me?
I can't say, Signora. I follow orders.
Fine.
In this house, I give the orders.

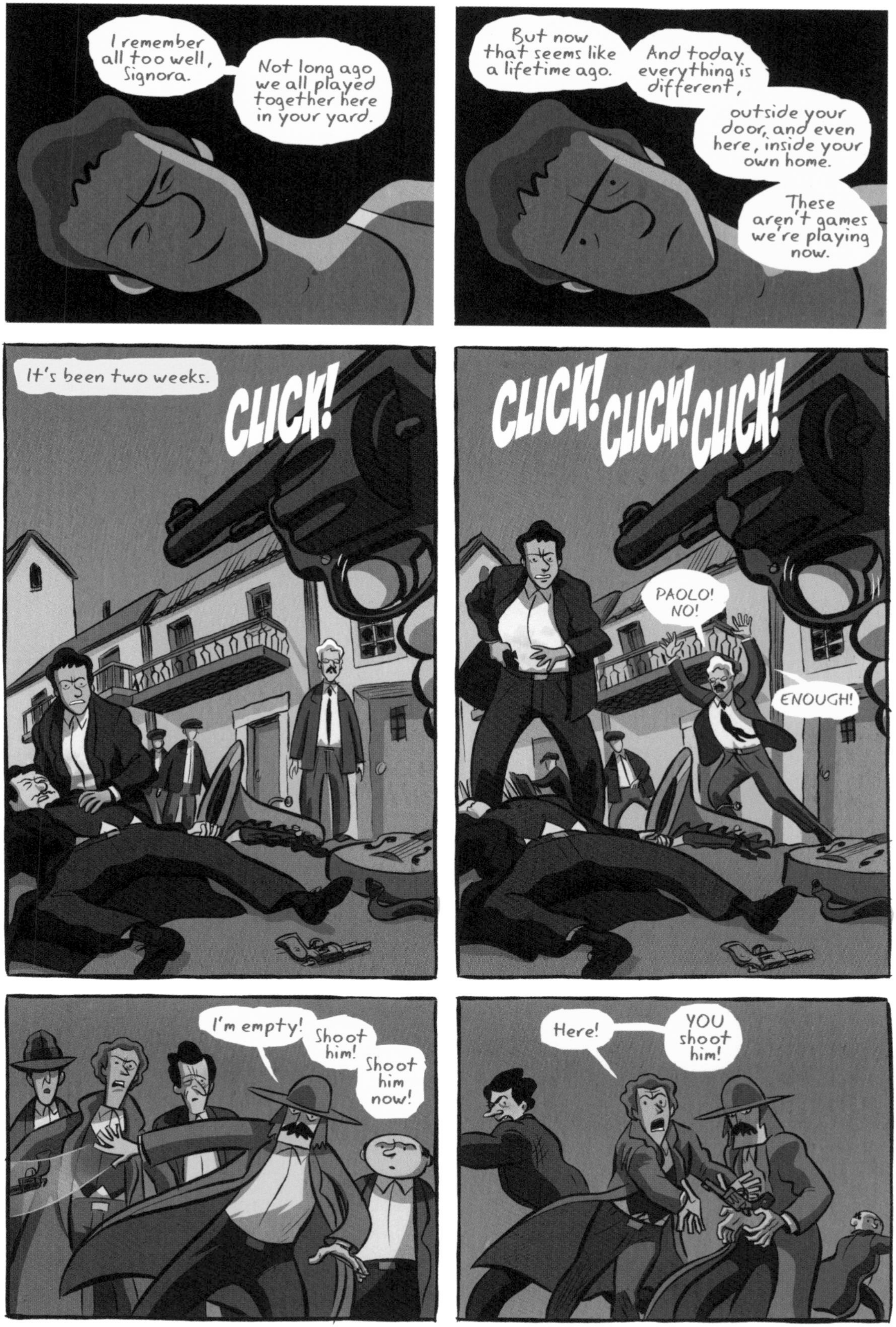
I remember all too well, Signora.
Not long ago we all played together here in your yard.
But now that seems like a lifetime ago.
And today everything is different,
outside your door, and even here, inside your own home.
These aren't games we're playing now.
It's been two weeks.
CLICK!
CLICK! CLICK! CLICK!
PAOLO! NO!
ENOUGH!
I'm empty!
Shoot him!
Shoot him now!
Here!
YOU shoot him!

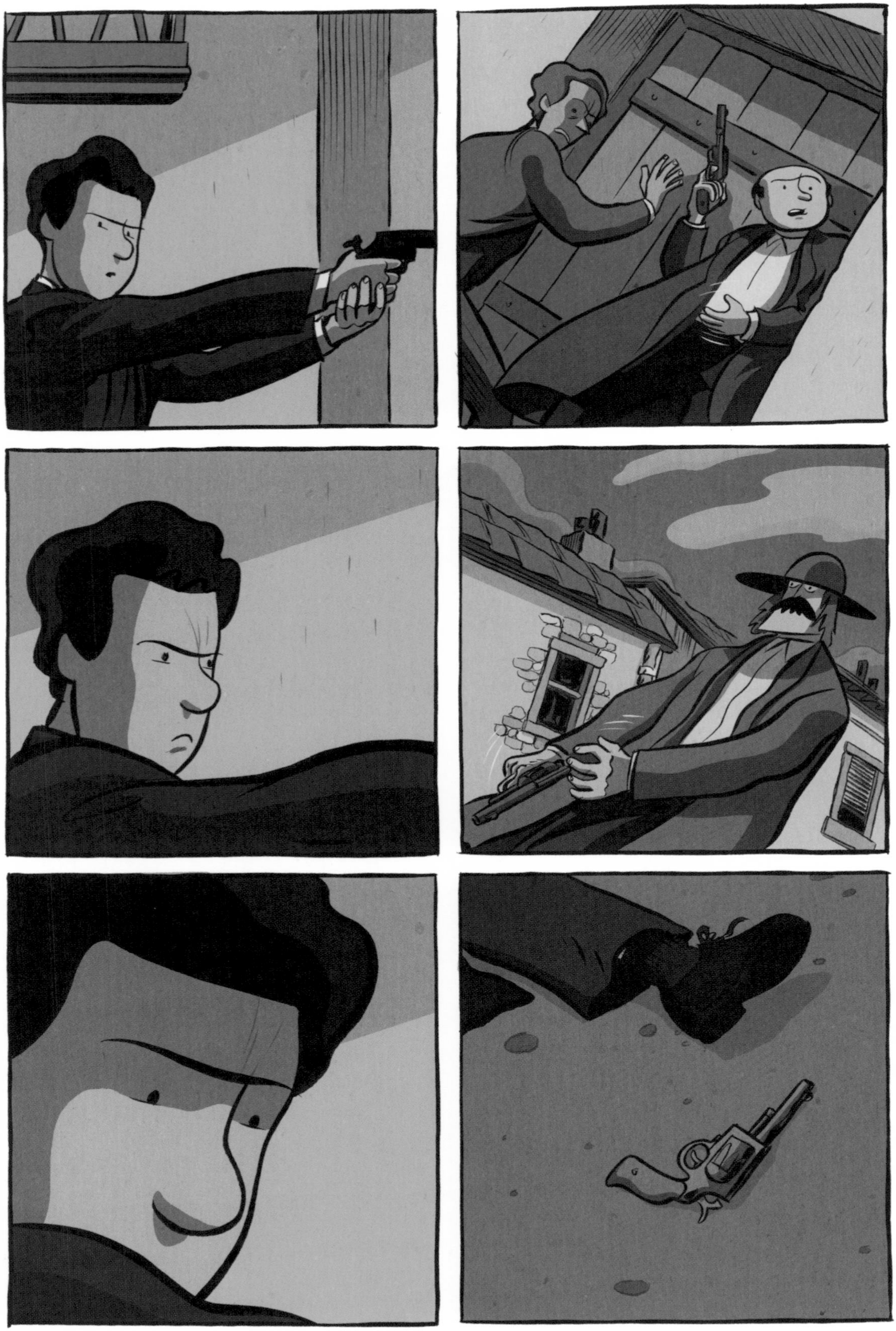

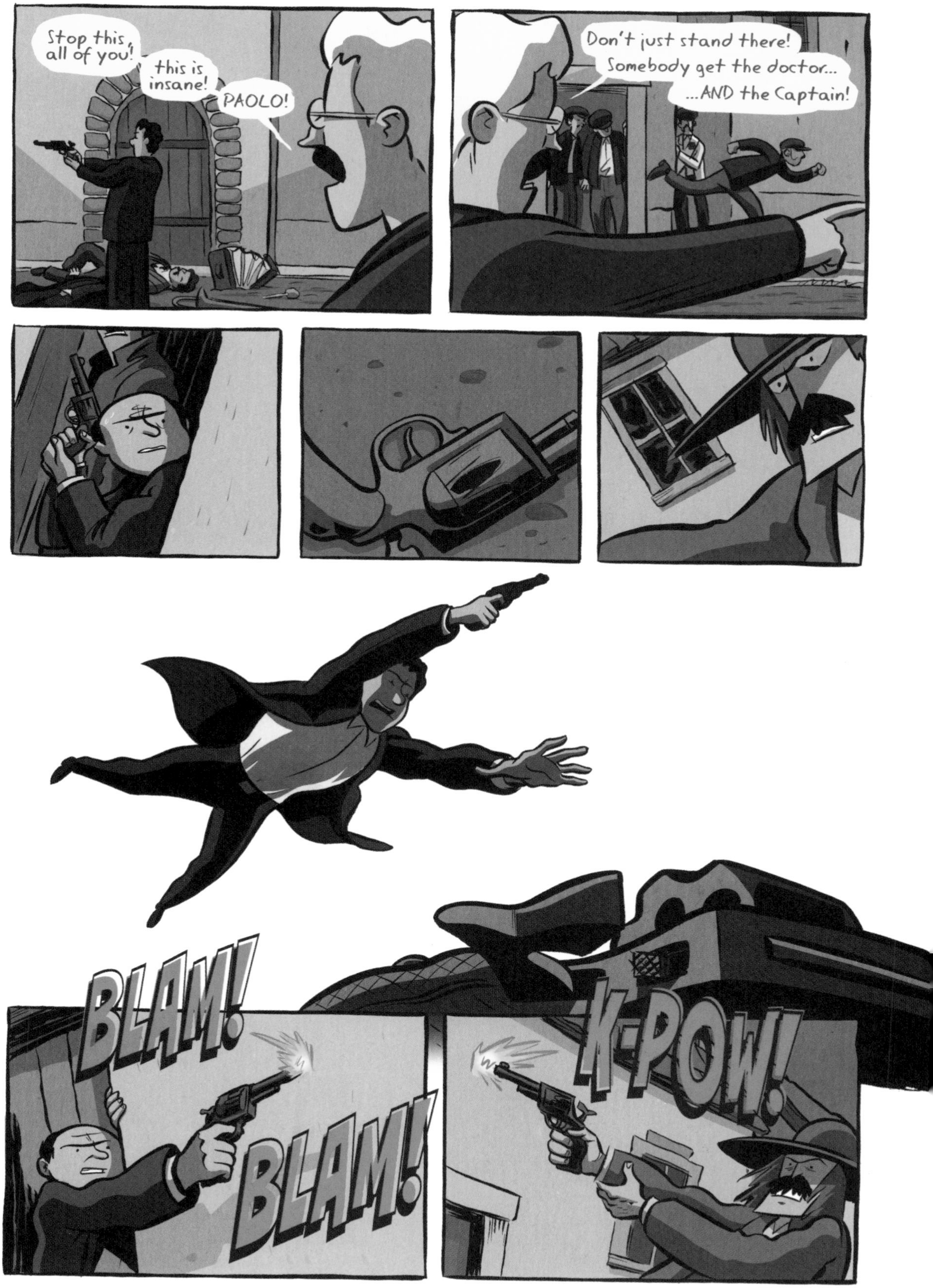
Stop this, all of you!
this is insane!
PAOLO!
Don't just stand there!
Somebody get the doctor...
...AND the Captain!
BLAM!
BLAM!
K-POW!

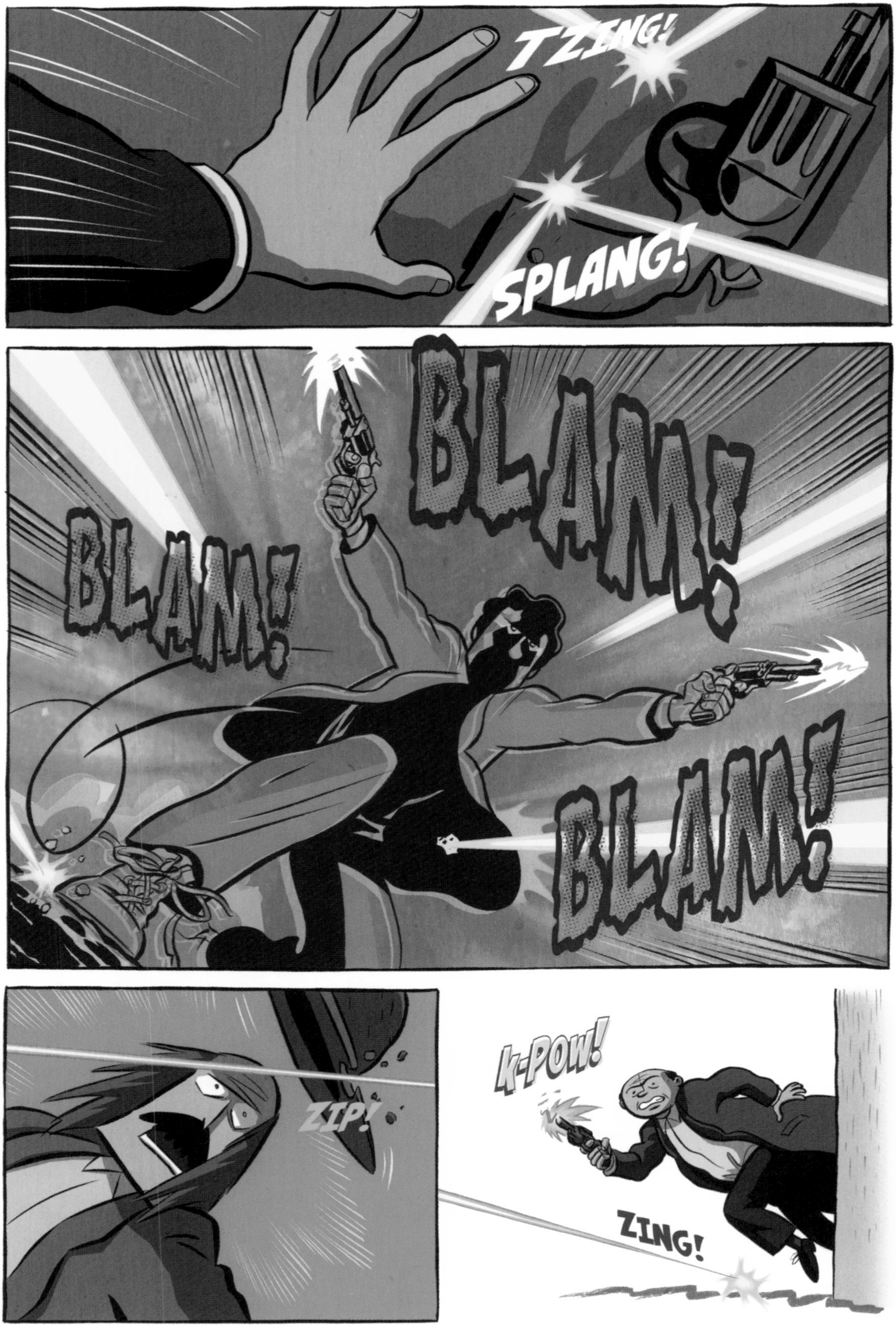
TZING!
SPLANG!
BLAM!
BLAM!
BLAM!
ZIP!
K-POW!
ZING!

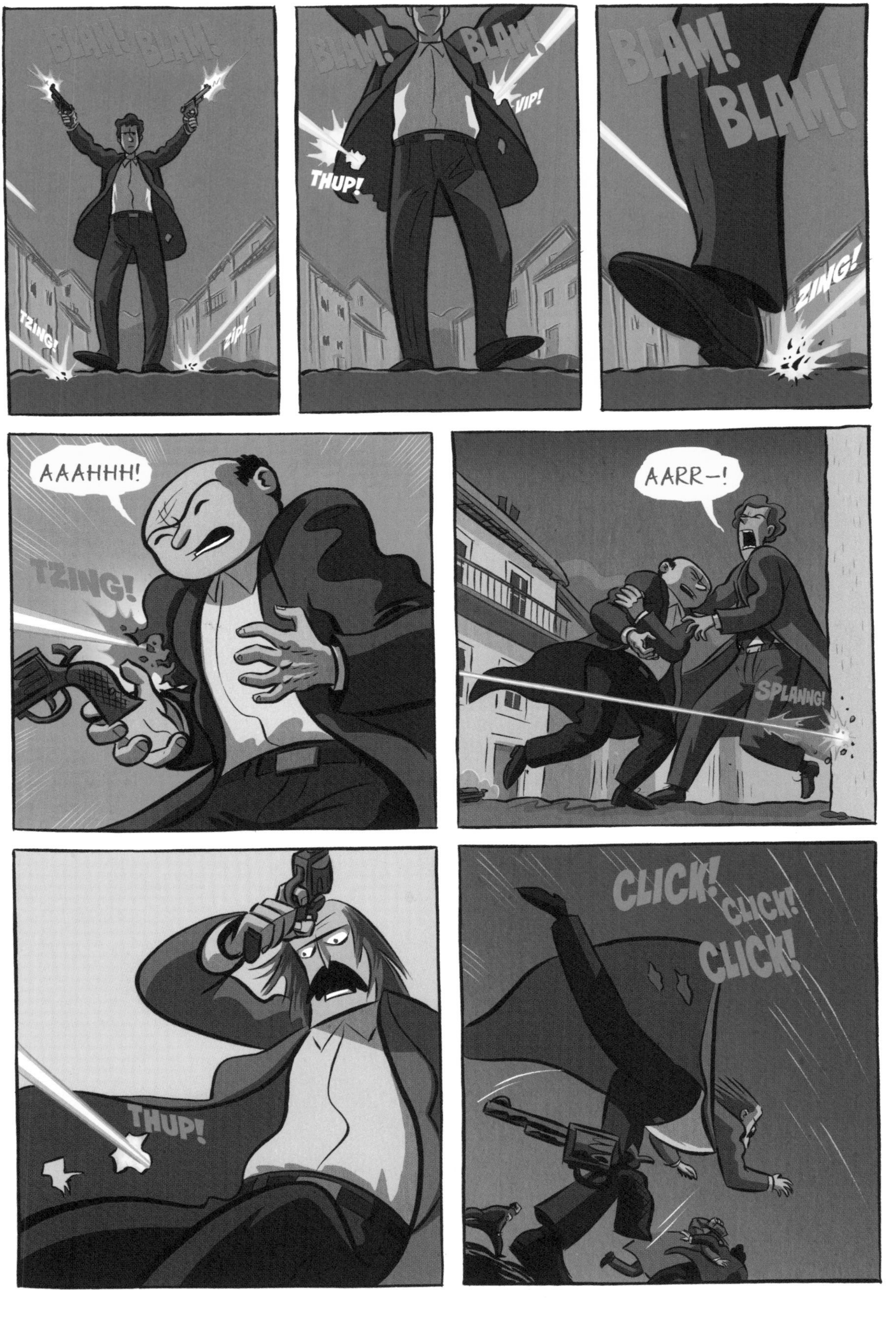
BLAM! BLAM!
TZING!
ZIP!
BLAM! BLAM!
VIP!
THUP!
BLAM! BLAM!
ZING!
AAAHHH!
TZING!
AARR—!
SPLANNG!
THUP!
CLICK! CLICK! CLICK!

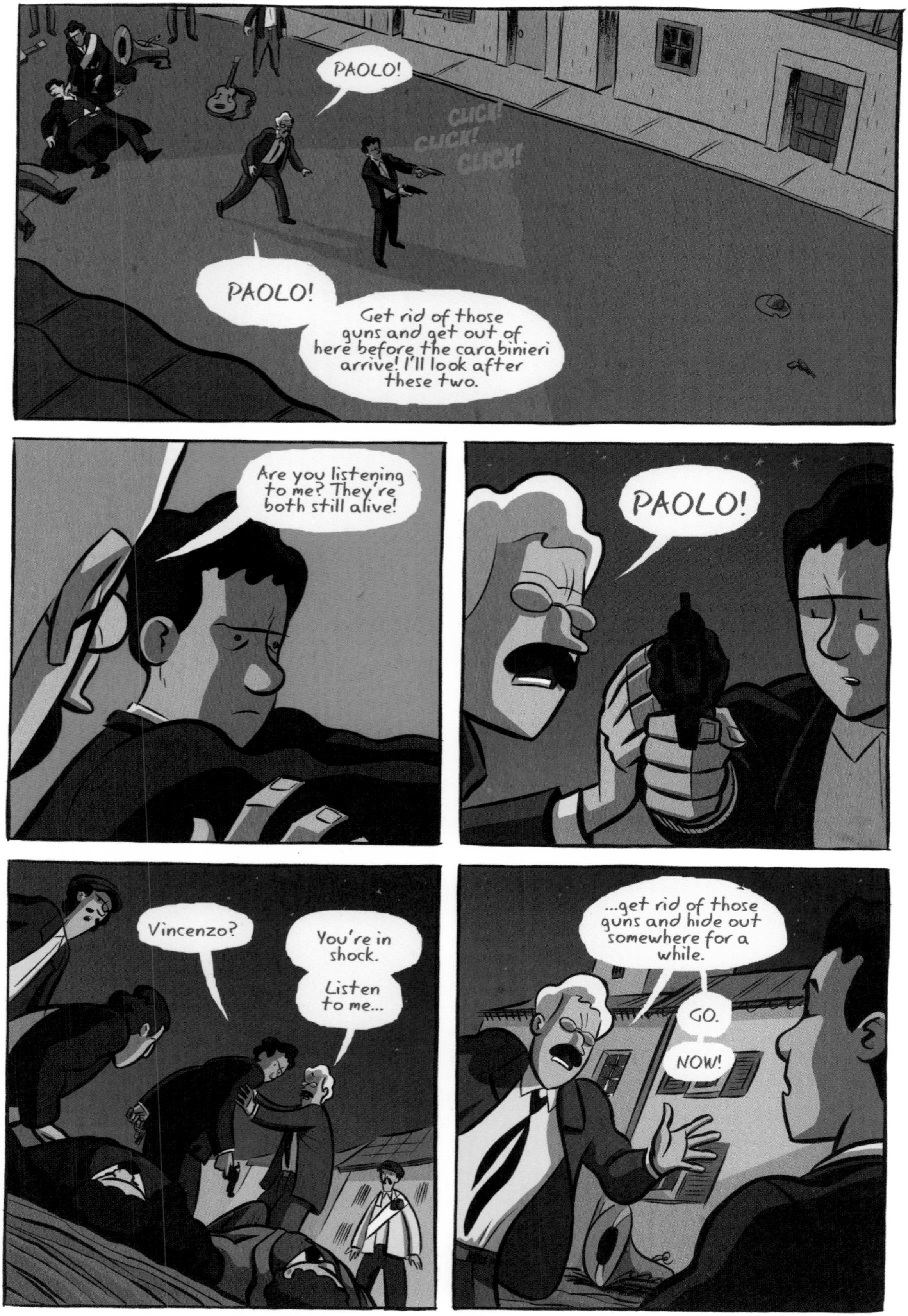
PAOLO!
CLICK! CLICK! CLICK!
PAOLO!
Get rid of those guns and get out of here before the carabinieri arrive! I'll look after these two.
Are you listening to me? They're both still alive!
PAOLO!
Vincenzo?
You're in shock.
Listen to me...
...get rid of those guns and hide out somewhere for a while.
GO.
NOW!

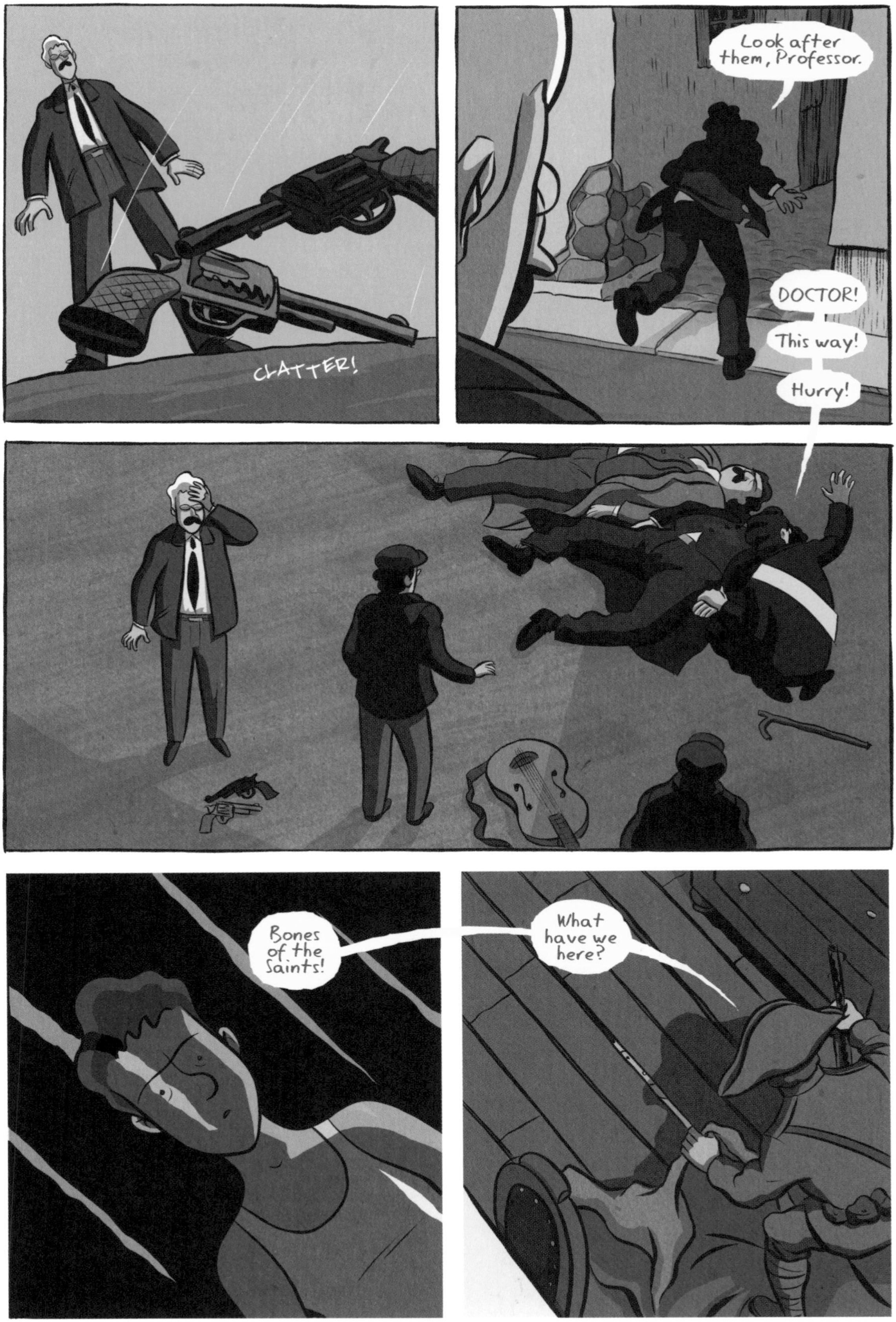
CLATTER!
Look after them, Professor.
DOCTOR!
This way!
Hurry!
Bones of the Saints!
What have we here?

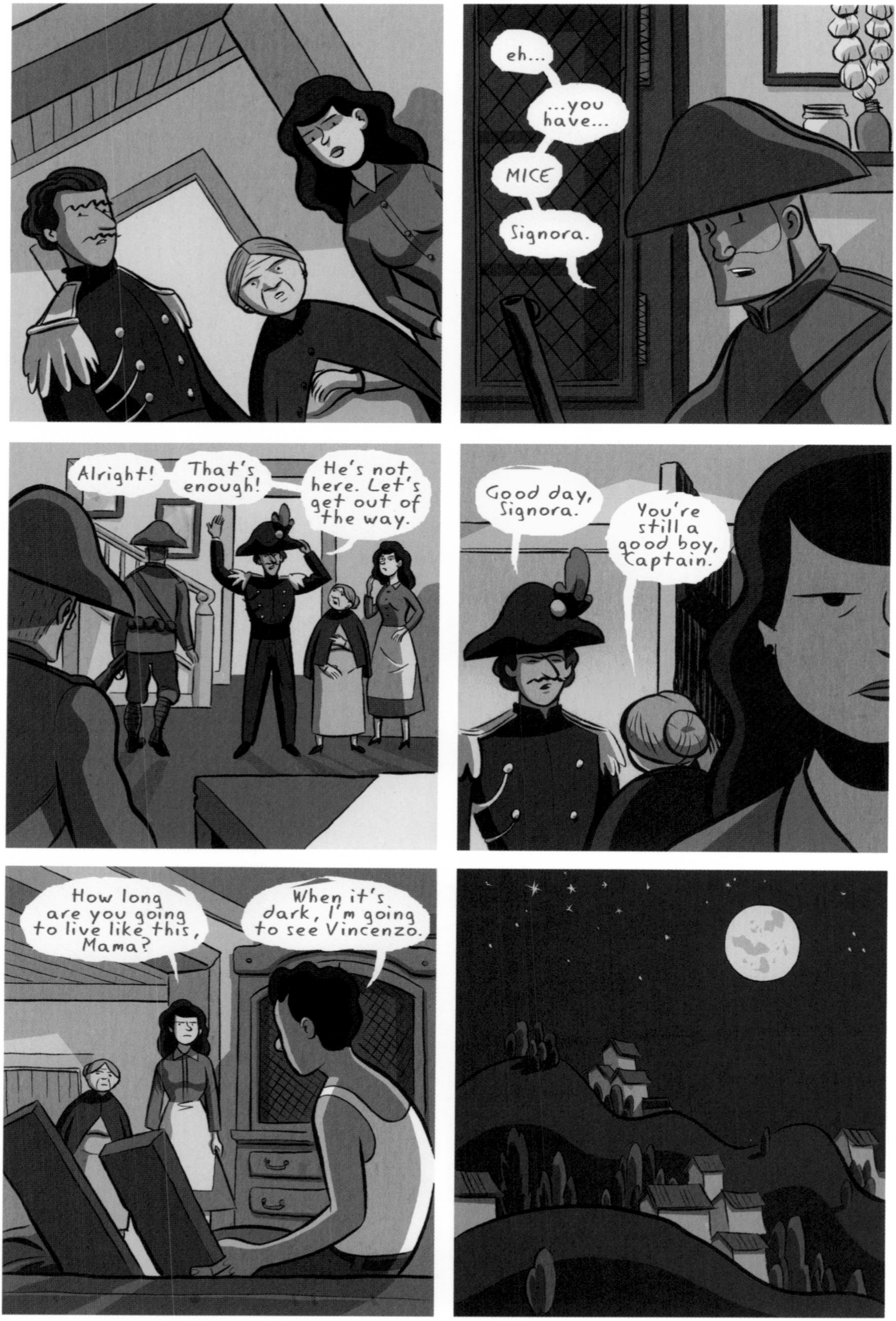
eh...
...you have...
MICE
Signora.
Alright!
That's enough!
He's not here. Let's get out of the way.
Good day, Signora.
You're still a good boy, Captain.
How long are you going to live like this, Mama?
When it's dark, I'm going to see Vincenzo.

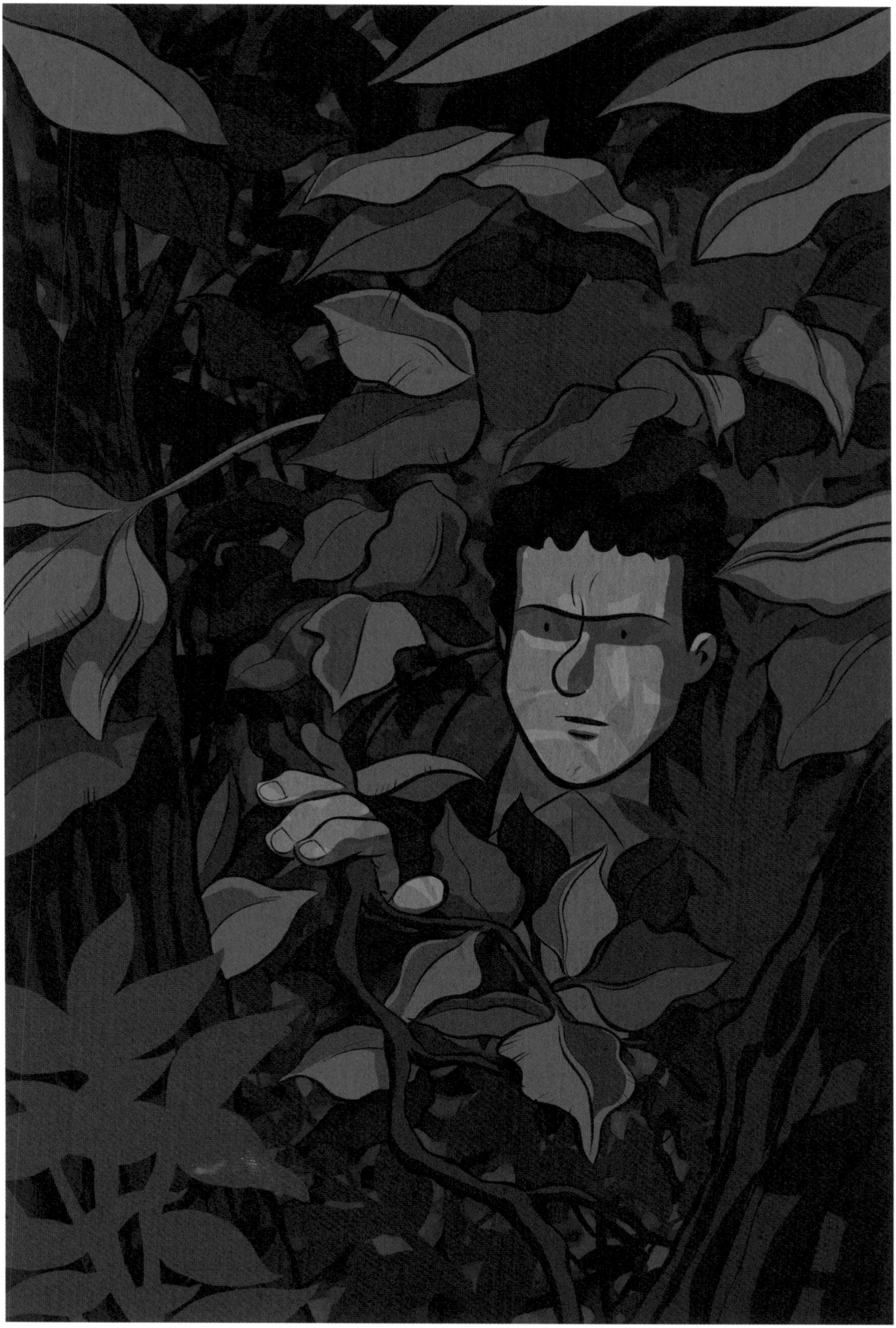

Of course they knew I'd try to see him.

But Salvatore and Pino had both slept their way through school, and this night was no different.

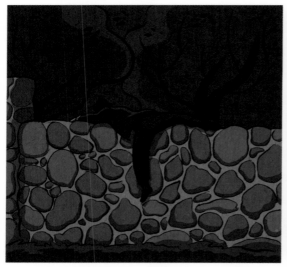

Zzzzzzzz

And soon there we were.

Together again.

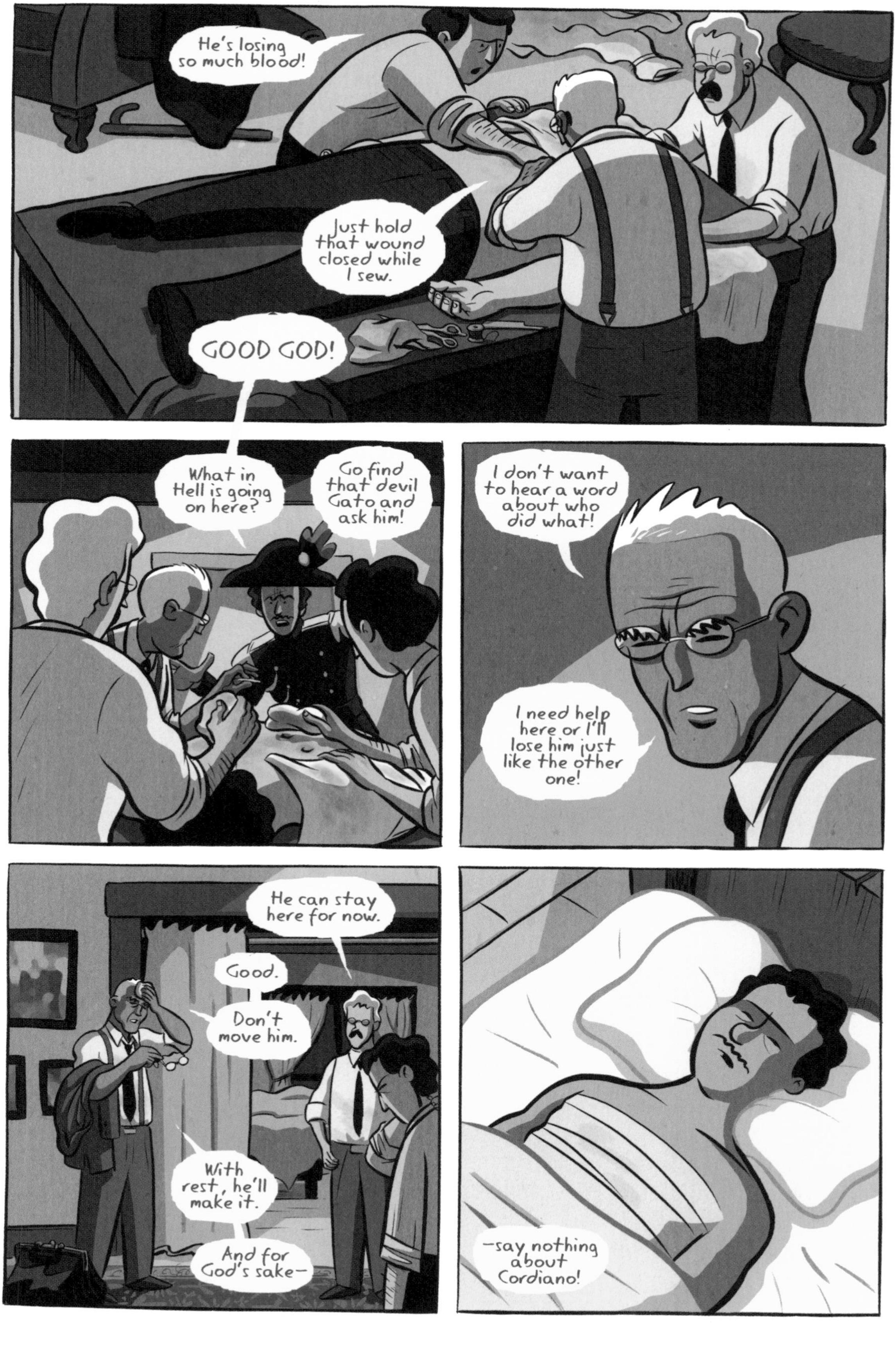
He's losing so much blood!
Just hold that wound closed while I sew.
GOOD GOD!
What in Hell is going on here?
Go find that devil Gato and ask him!
I don't want to hear a word about who did what!
I need help here or I'll lose him just like the other one!
He can stay here for now.
Good.
Don't move him.
With rest, he'll make it.
And for God's sake—
—say nothing about Cordiano!

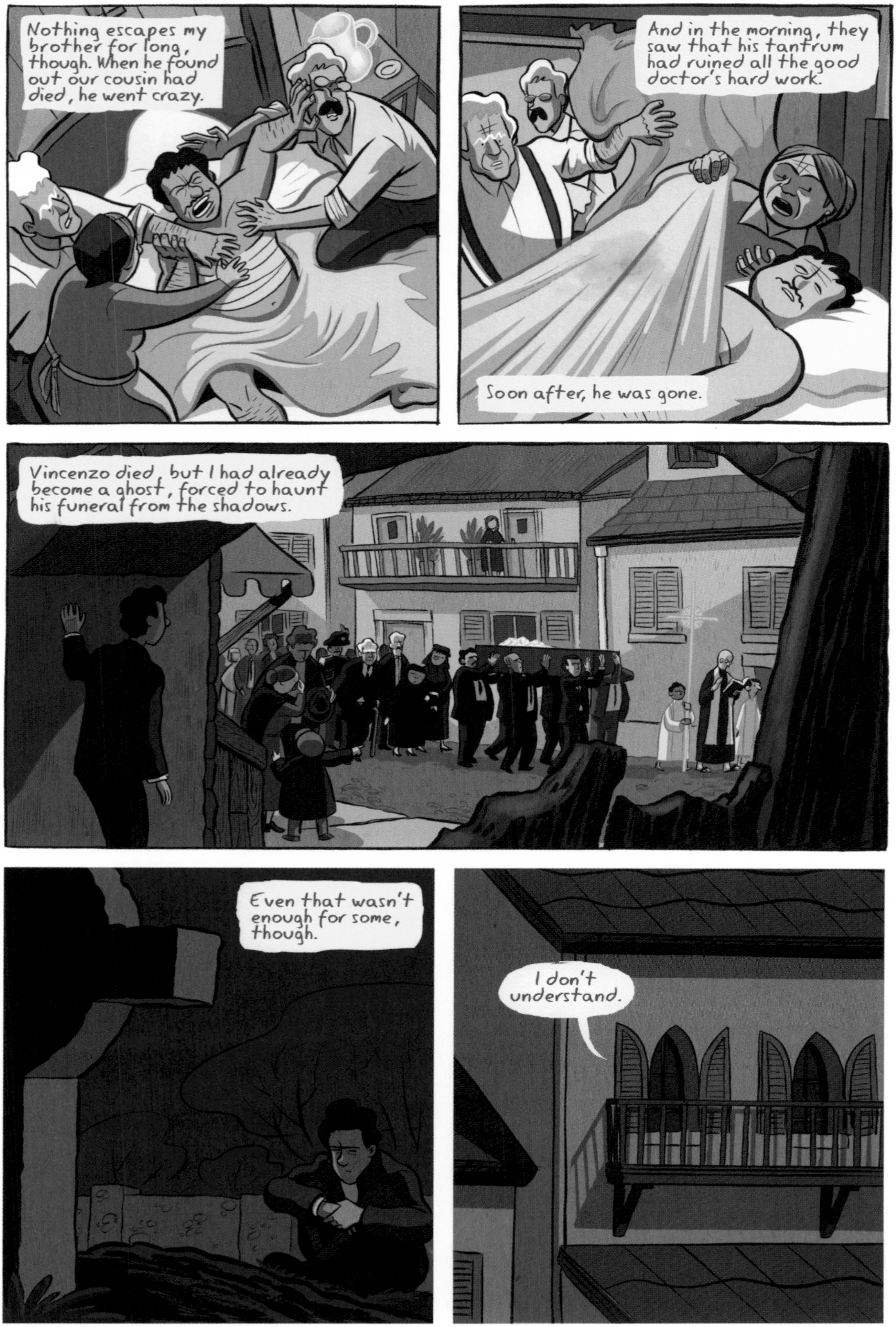
Nothing escapes my brother for long, though. When he found out our cousin had died, he went crazy.
And in the morning, they saw that his tantrum had ruined all the good doctor's hard work.
Soon after, he was gone.
Vincenzo died, but I had already become a ghost, forced to haunt his funeral from the shadows.
Even that wasn't enough for some, though.
I don't understand.

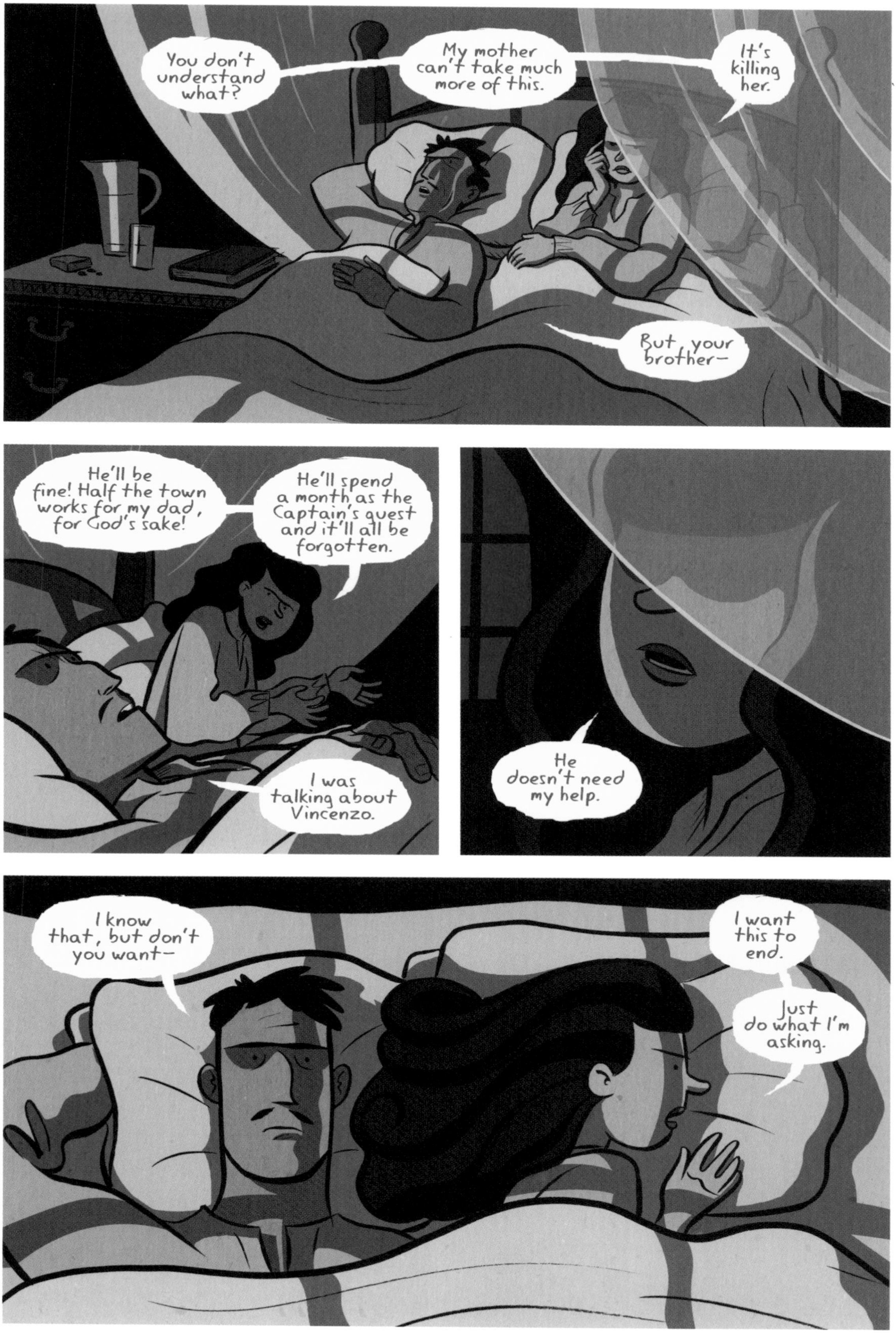
You don't understand what?
My mother can't take much more of this.
It's killing her.
But, your brother—
He'll be fine! Half the town works for my dad, for God's sake!
He'll spend a month as the Captain's guest and it'll all be forgotten.
I was talking about Vincenzo.
He doesn't need my help.
I know that, but don't you want—
I want this to end.
Just do what I'm asking.

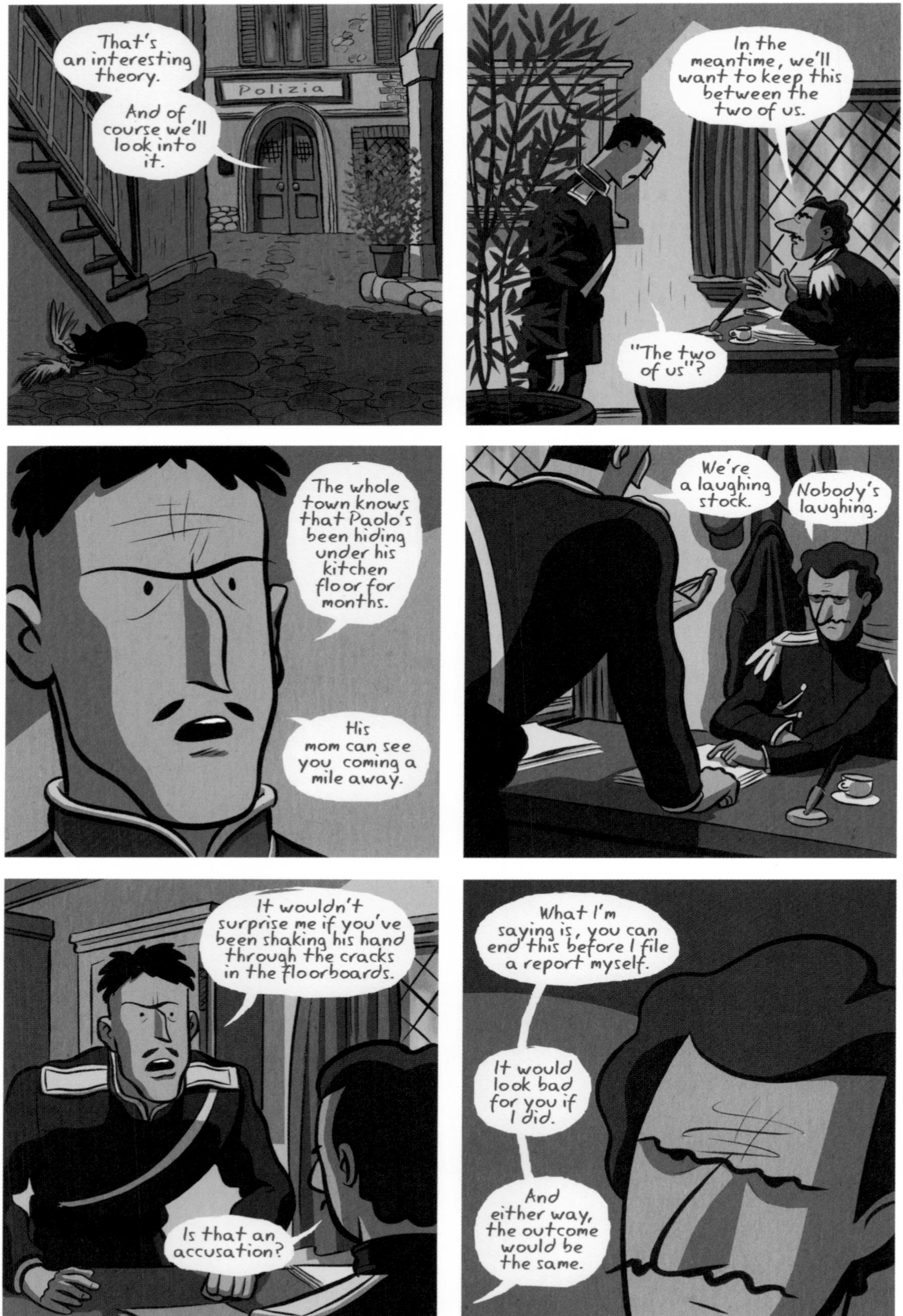
That's an interesting theory.
And of course we'll look into it.
Polizia
In the meantime, we'll want to keep this between the two of us.
"The two of us"?
The whole town knows that Paolo's been hiding under his kitchen floor for months.
His mom can see you coming a mile away.
We're a laughing stock.
Nobody's laughing.
It wouldn't surprise me if you've been shaking his hand through the cracks in the floorboards.
Is that an accusation?
What I'm saying is, you can end this before I file a report myself.
It would look bad for you if I did.
And either way, the outcome would be the same.

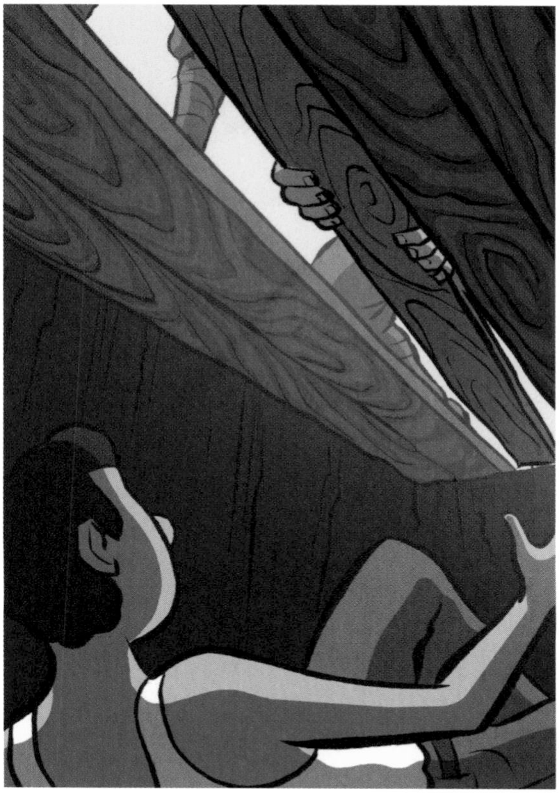

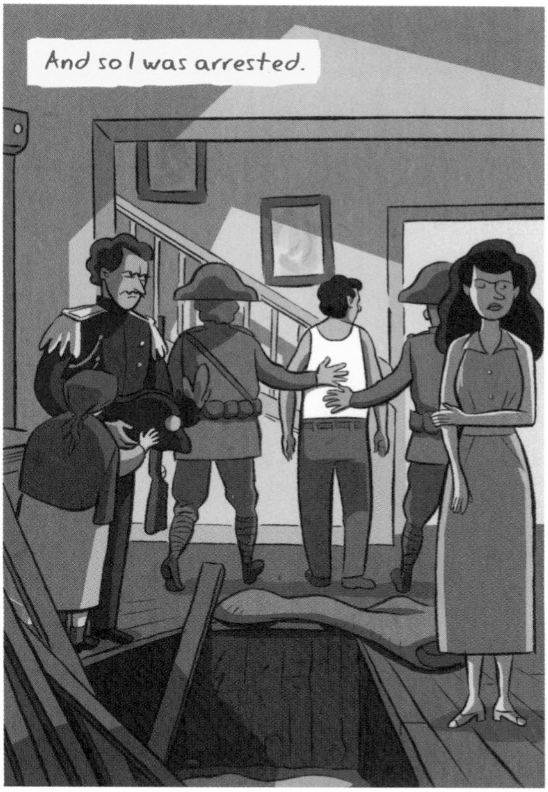
And so I was arrested.

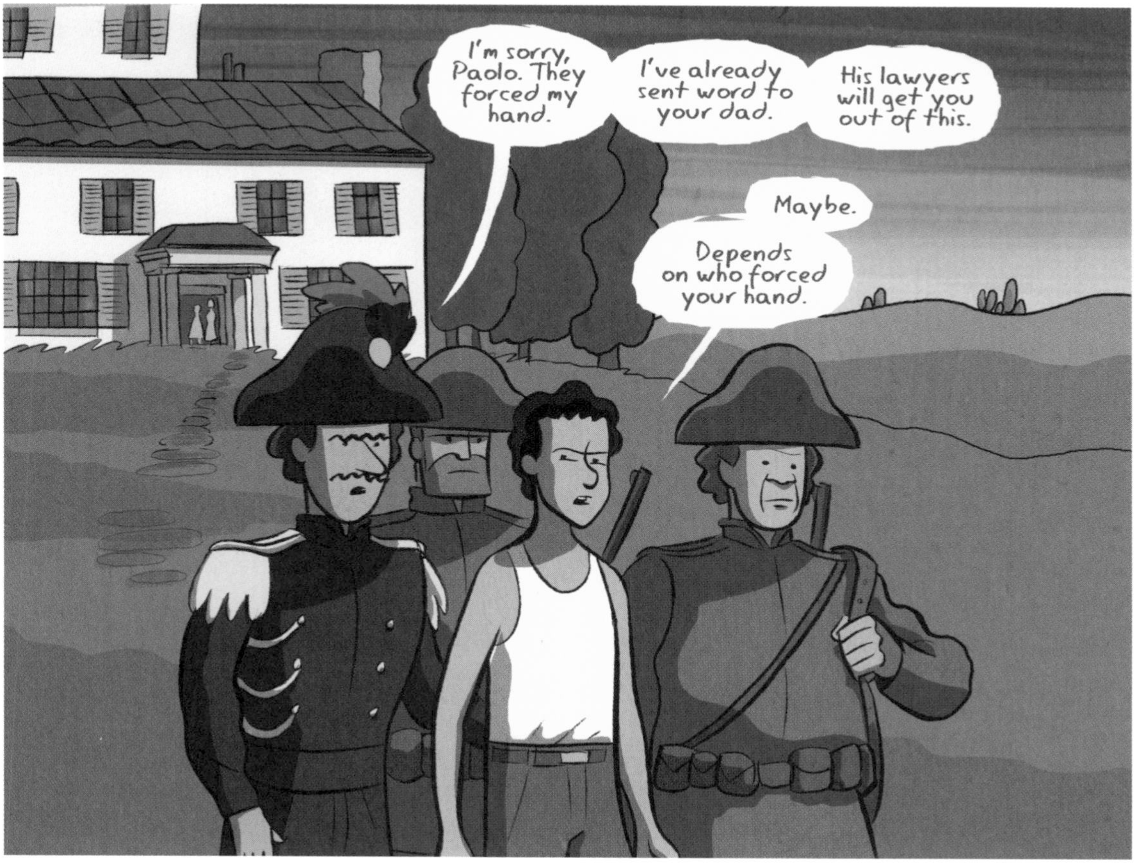
I'm sorry, Paolo. They forced my hand.
I've already sent word to your dad.
His lawyers will get you out of this.
Maybe.
Depends on who forced your hand.

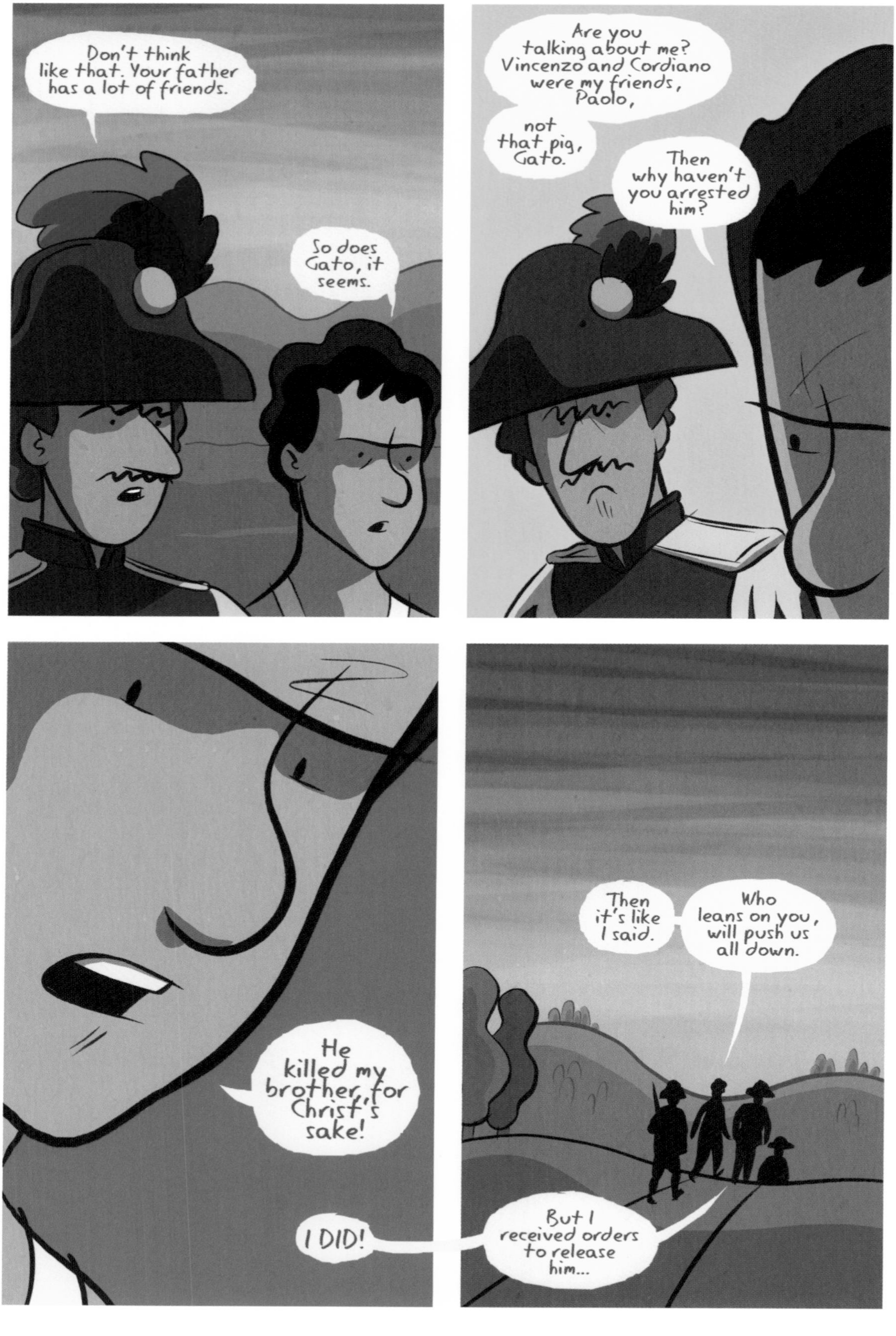
Don't think like that. Your father has a lot of friends.
So does Gato, it seems.
Are you talking about me? Vincenzo and Cordiano were my friends, Paolo,
not that pig, Gato.
Then why haven't you arrested him?
He killed my brother, for Christ's sake!
I DID!
But I received orders to release him...
Then it's like I said.
Who leans on you, will push us all down.

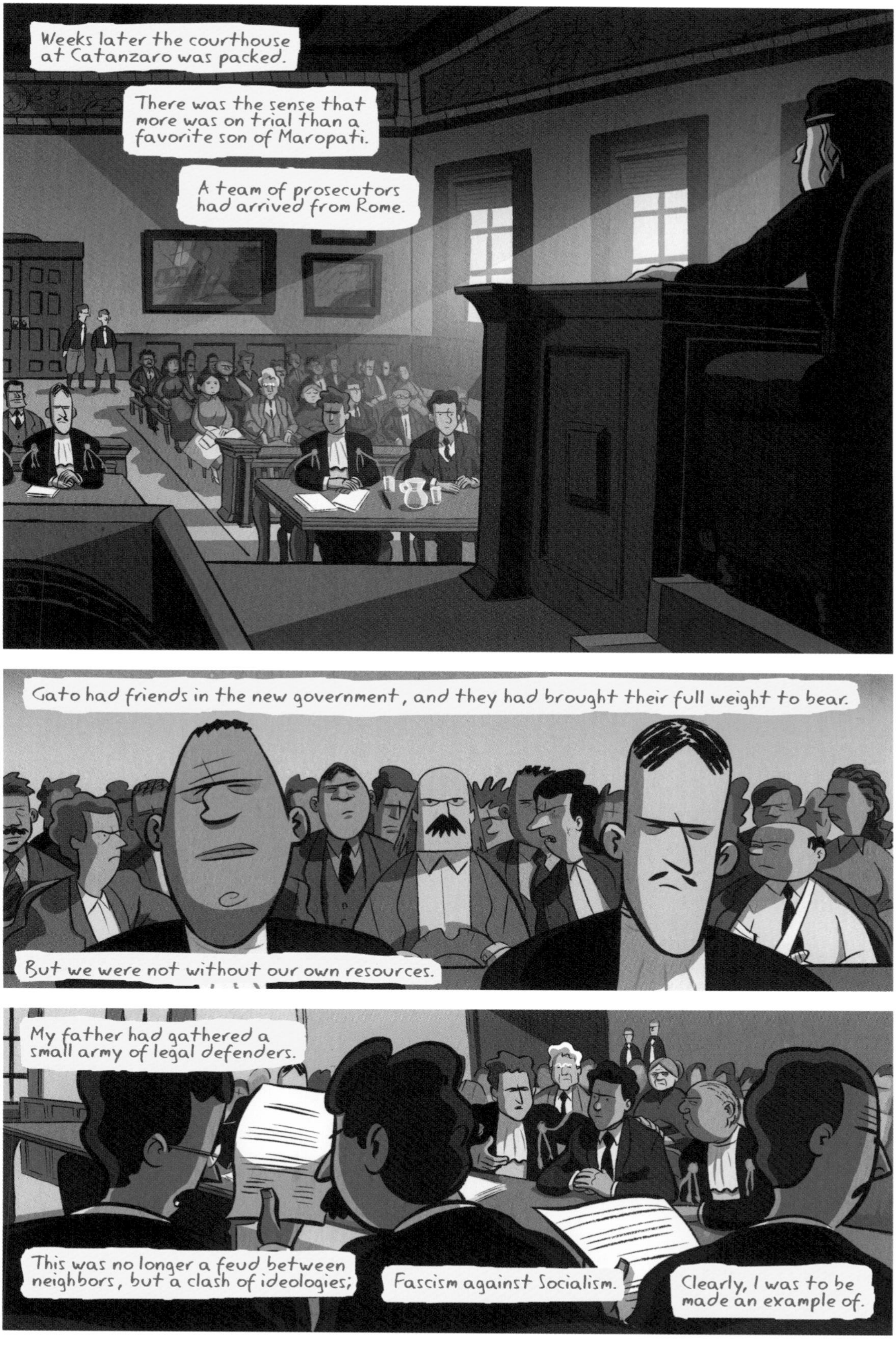
Weeks later the courthouse at Catanzaro was packed.
There was the sense that more was on trial than a favorite son of Maropati.
A team of prosecutors had arrived from Rome.
Gato had friends in the new government, and they had brought their full weight to bear.
But we were not without our own resources.
My father had gathered a small army of legal defenders.
This was no longer a feud between neighbors, but a clash of ideologies;
Fascism against Socialism.
Clearly, I was to be made an example of.

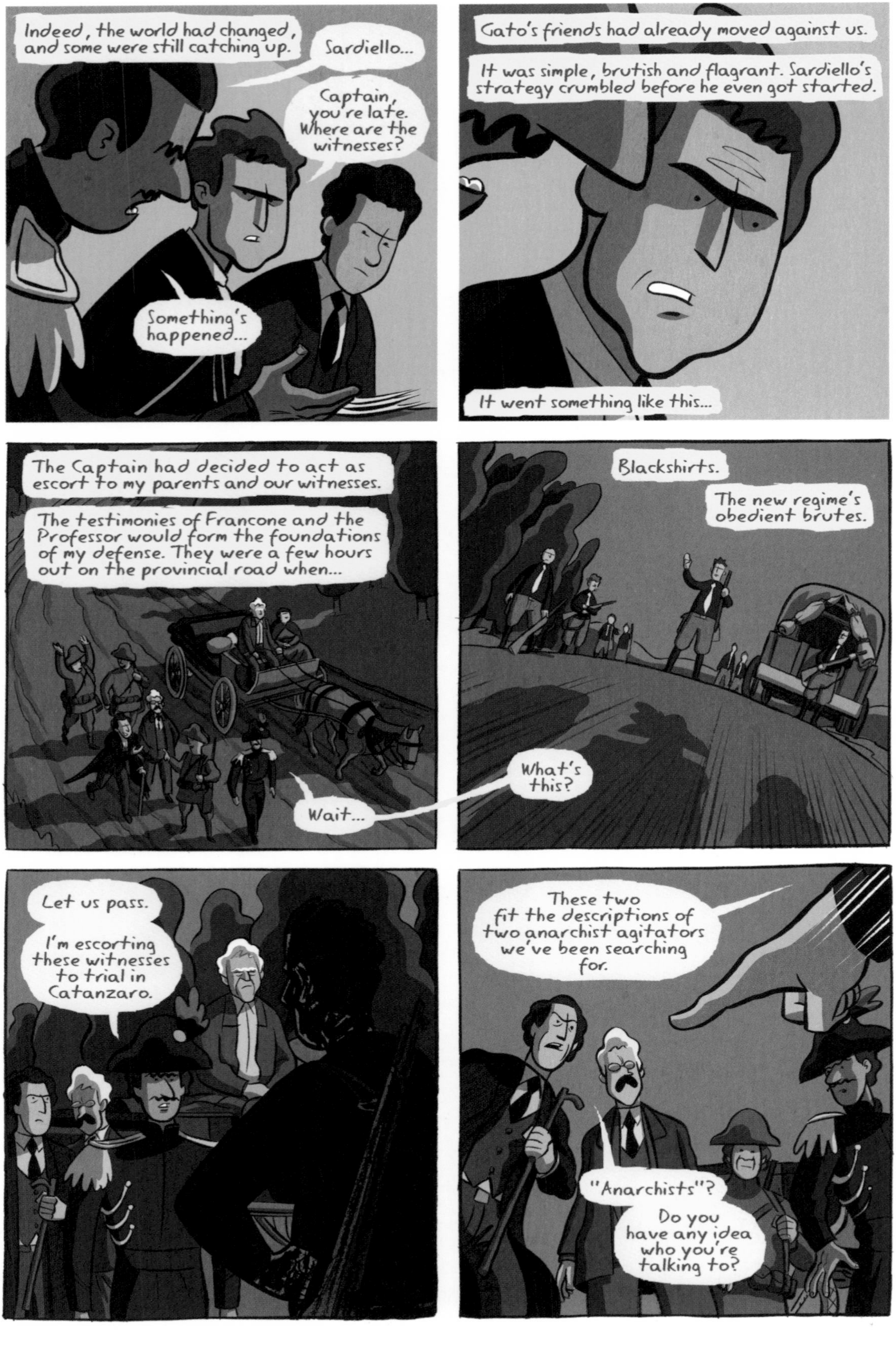
Indeed, the world had changed, and some were still catching up.
Sardiello...
Captain, you're late. Where are the witnesses?
Something's happened...
Gato's friends had already moved against us.
It was simple, brutish and flagrant. Sardiello's strategy crumbled before he even got started.
It went something like this...
The Captain had decided to act as escort to my parents and our witnesses.
The testimonies of Francone and the Professor would form the foundations of my defense. They were a few hours out on the provincial road when...
Wait...
Blackshirts.
The new regime's obedient brutes.
What's this?
Let us pass.
I'm escorting these witnesses to trial in Catanzaro.
These two fit the descriptions of two anarchist agitators we've been searching for.
"Anarchists"?
Do you have any idea who you're talking to?

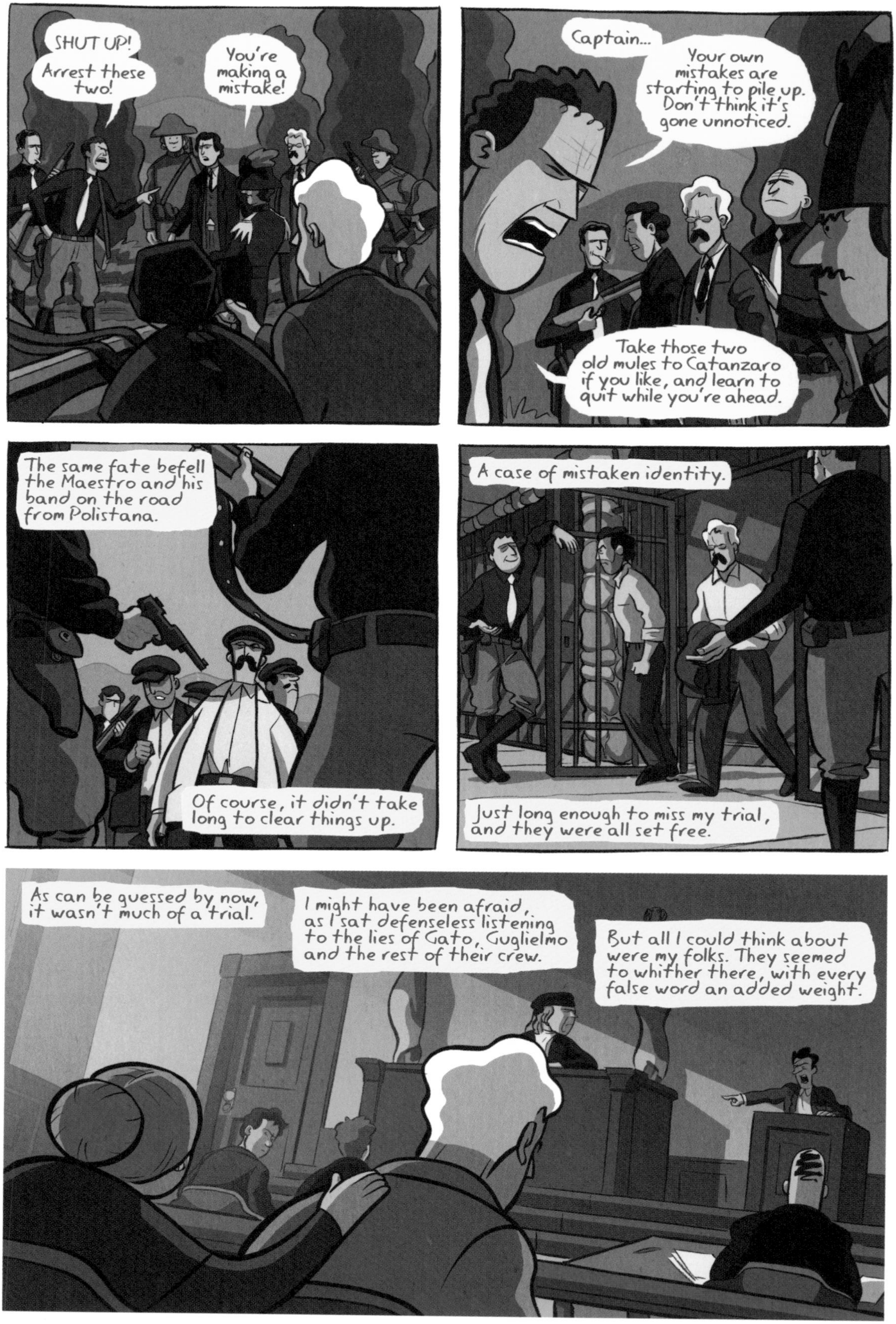
SHUT UP! Arrest these two!
You're making a mistake!
Captain...
Your own mistakes are starting to pile up. Don't think it's gone unnoticed.
Take those two old mules to Catanzaro if you like, and learn to quit while you're ahead.
The same fate befell the Maestro and his band on the road from Polistana.
Of course, it didn't take long to clear things up.
A case of mistaken identity.
Just long enough to miss my trial, and they were all set free.
As can be guessed by now, it wasn't much of a trial.
I might have been afraid, as I sat defenseless listening to the lies of Gato, Guglielmo and the rest of their crew.
But all I could think about were my folks. They seemed to whither there, with every false word an added weight.

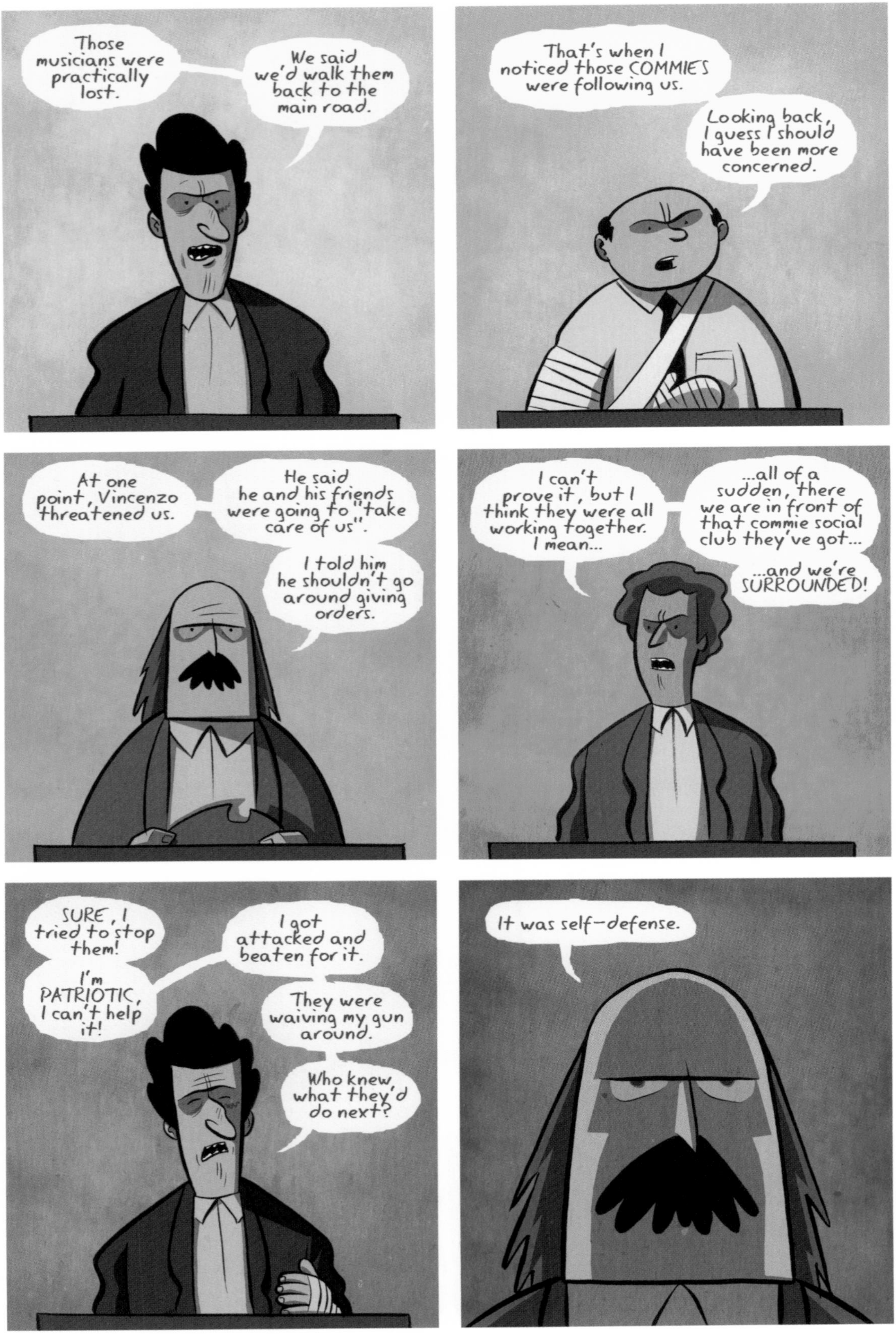
Those musicians were practically lost.
We said we'd walk them back to the main road.
That's when I noticed those COMMIES were following us.
Looking back, I guess I should have been more concerned.
At one point, Vincenzo threatened us.
He said he and his friends were going to "take care of us".
I told him he shouldn't go around giving orders.
I can't prove it, but I think they were all working together. I mean...
...all of a sudden, there we are in front of that commie social club they've got...
...and we're SURROUNDED!
SURE, I tried to stop them!
I'm PATRIOTIC, I can't help it!
I got attacked and beaten for it.
They were waiving my gun around.
Who knew what they'd do next?
It was self-defense.

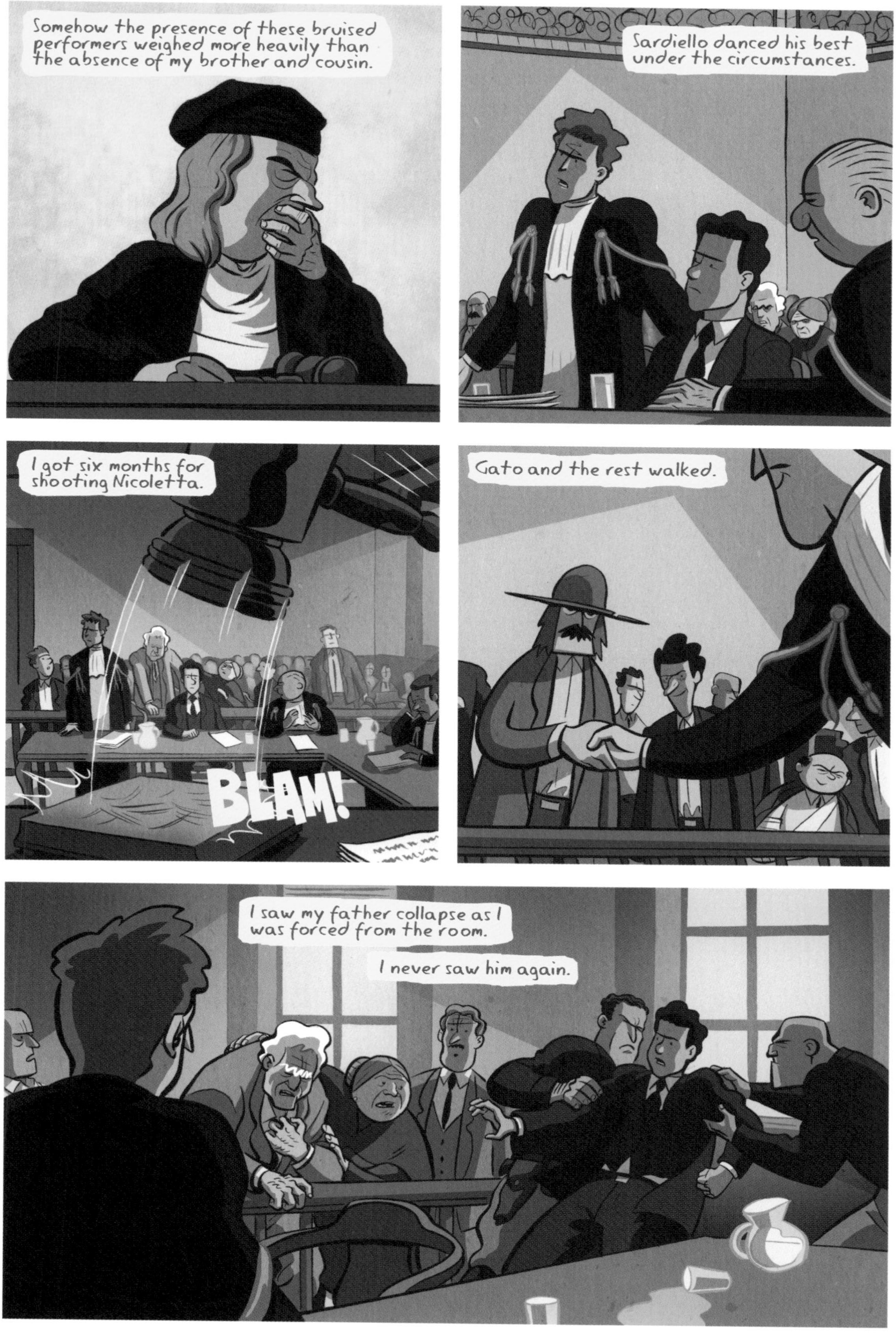
Somehow the presence of these bruised performers weighed more heavily than the absence of my brother and cousin.
Sardiello danced his best under the circumstances.
I got six months for shooting Nicoletta.
BLAM!
Gato and the rest walked.
I saw my father collapse as I was forced from the room.
I never saw him again.

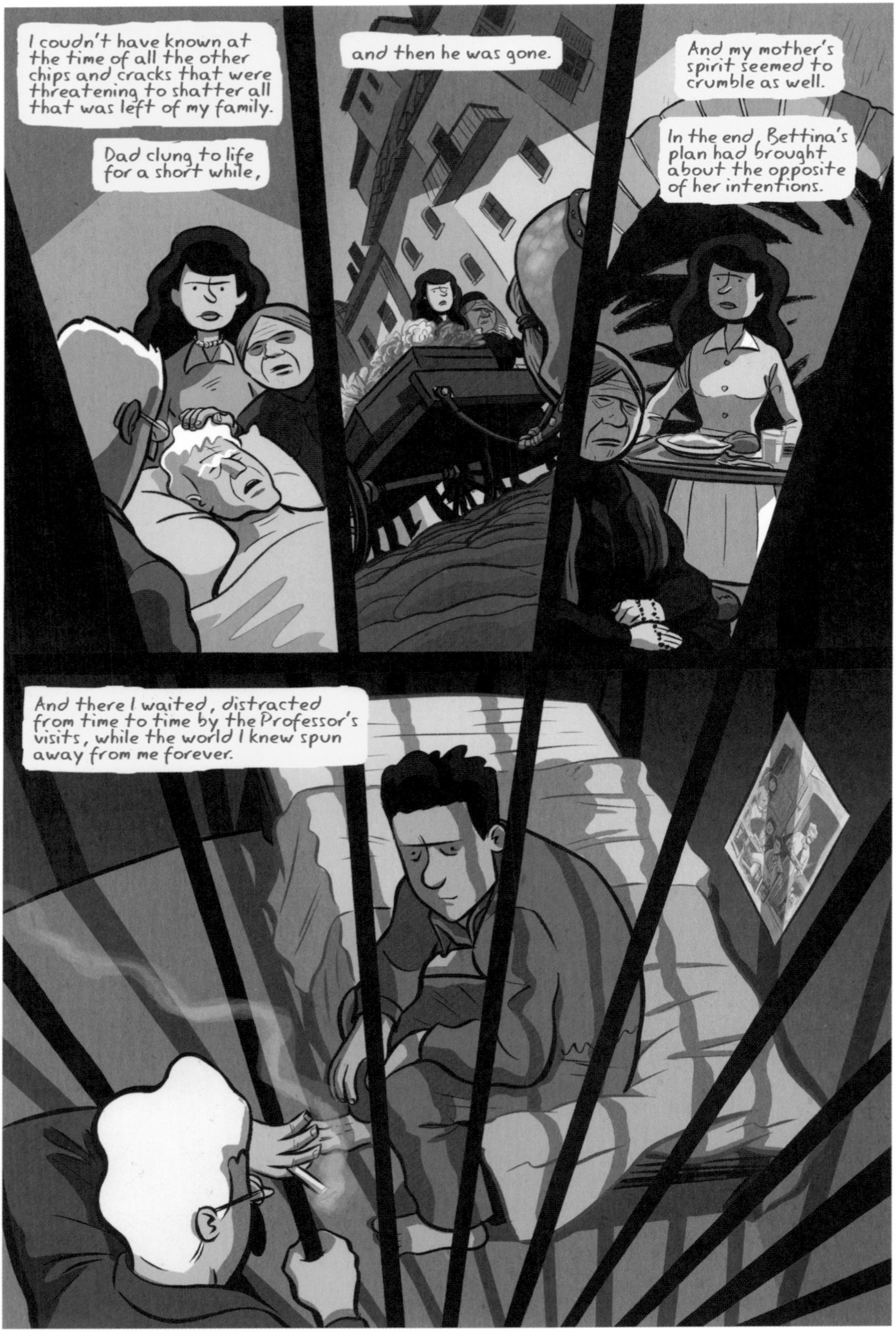
I coudn't have known at the time of all the other chips and cracks that were threatening to shatter all that was left of my family.
Dad clung to life for a short while,
and then he was gone.
And my mother's spirit seemed to crumble as well.
In the end, Bettina's plan had brought about the opposite of her intentions.
And there I waited, distracted from time to time by the Professor's visits, while the world I knew spun away from me forever.

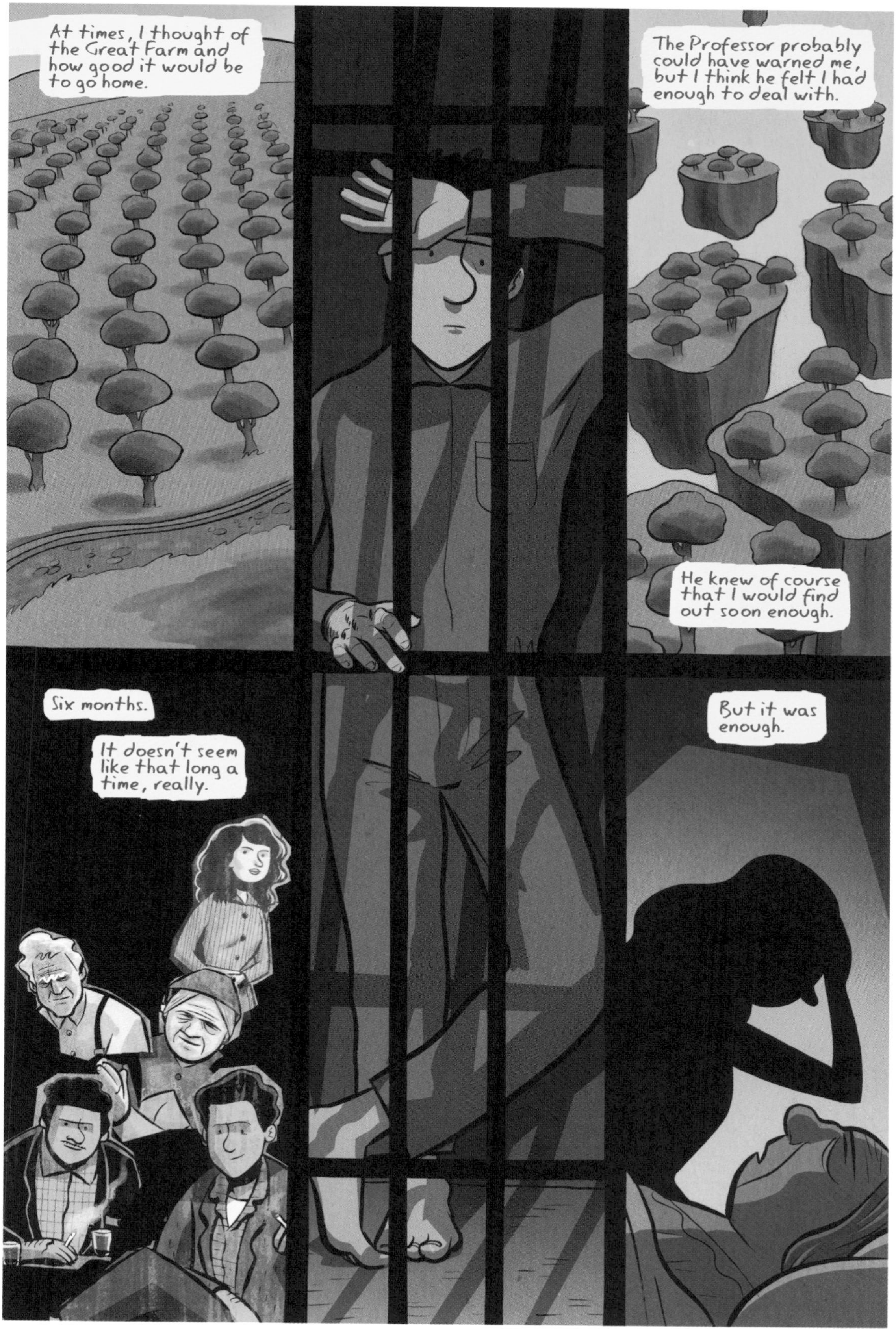
At times, I thought of the Great Farm and how good it would be to go home.
The Professor probably could have warned me, but I think he felt I had enough to deal with.
He knew of course that I would find out soon enough.
Six months.
It doesn't seem like that long a time, really.
But it was enough.

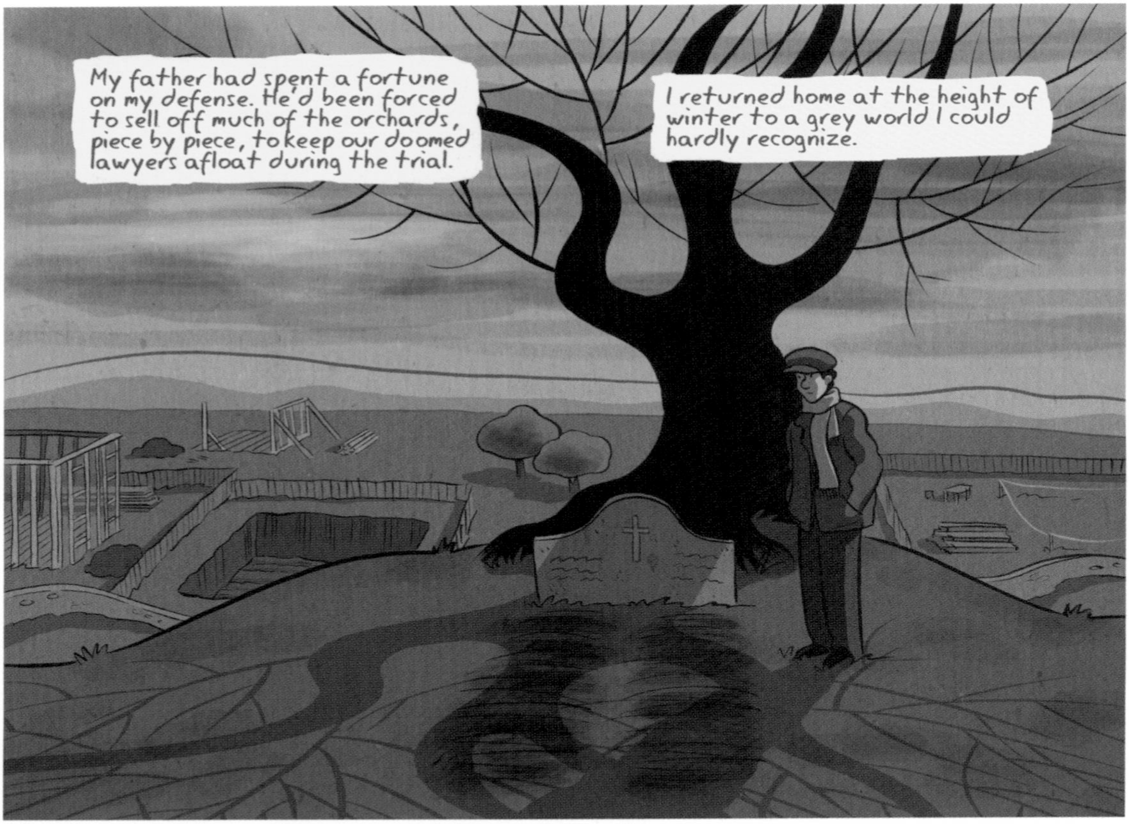
My father had spent a fortune on my defense. He'd been forced to sell off much of the orchards, piece by piece, to keep our doomed lawyers afloat during the trial.
I returned home at the height of winter to a grey world I could hardly recognize.

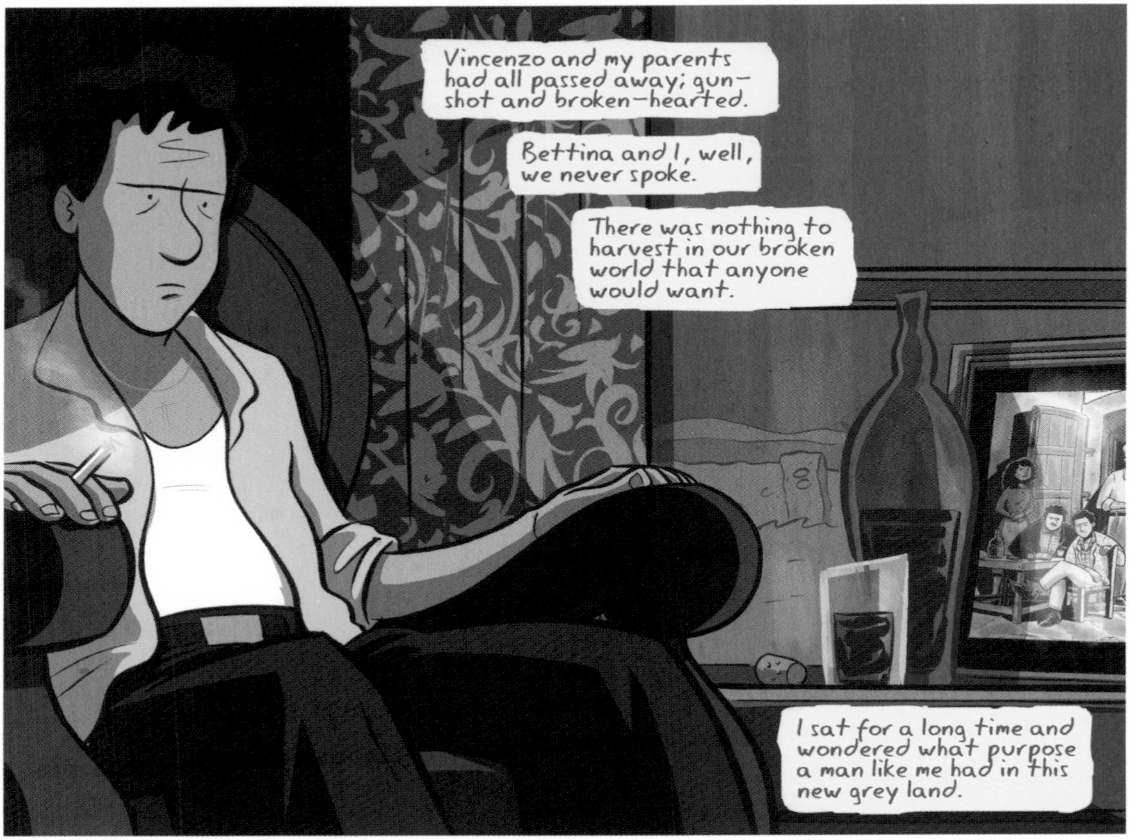
Vincenzo and my parents had all passed away; gun-shot and broken-hearted.
Bettina and I, well, we never spoke.
There was nothing to harvest in our broken world that anyone would want.
I sat for a long time and wondered what purpose a man like me had in this new grey land.

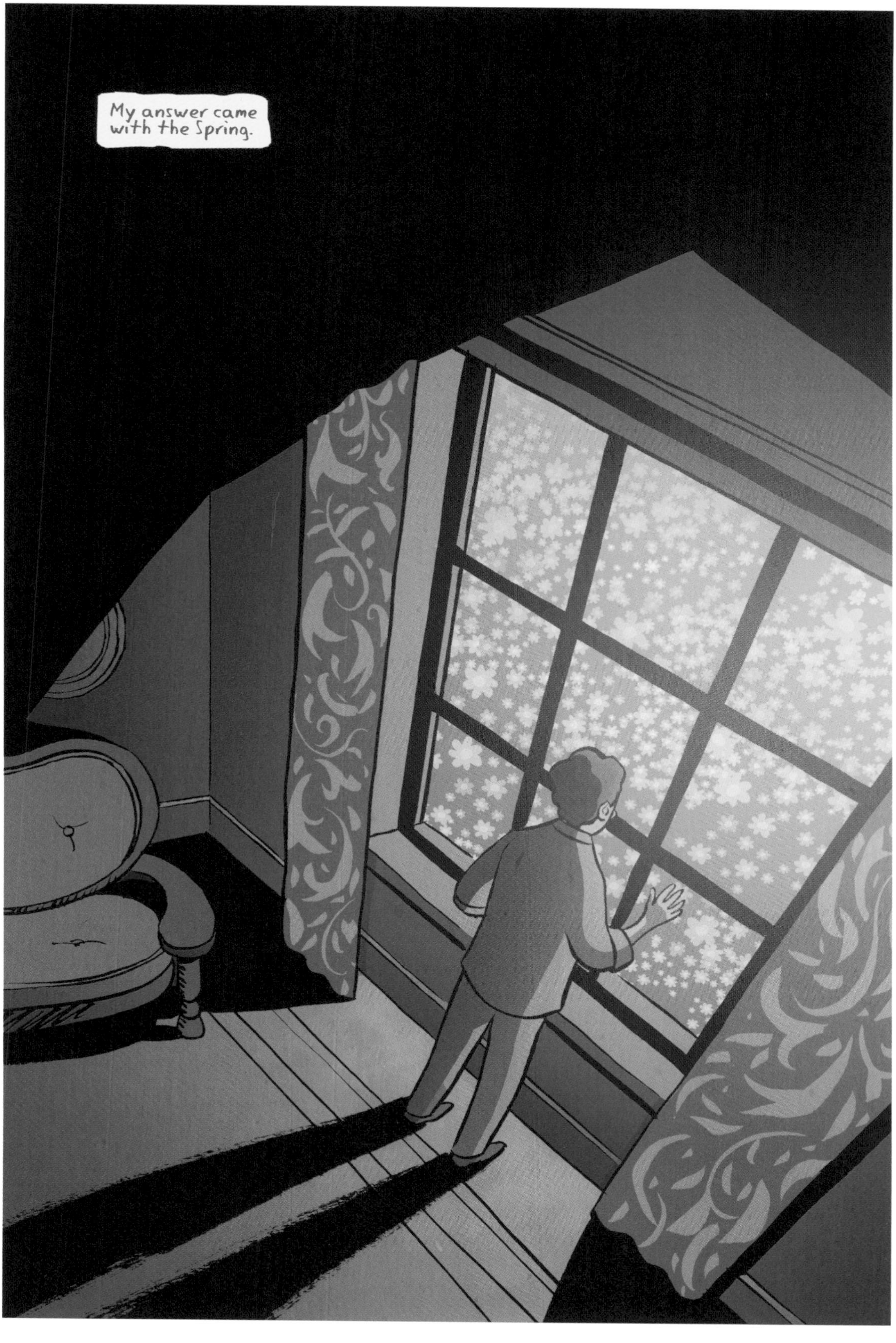
My answer came with the Spring.

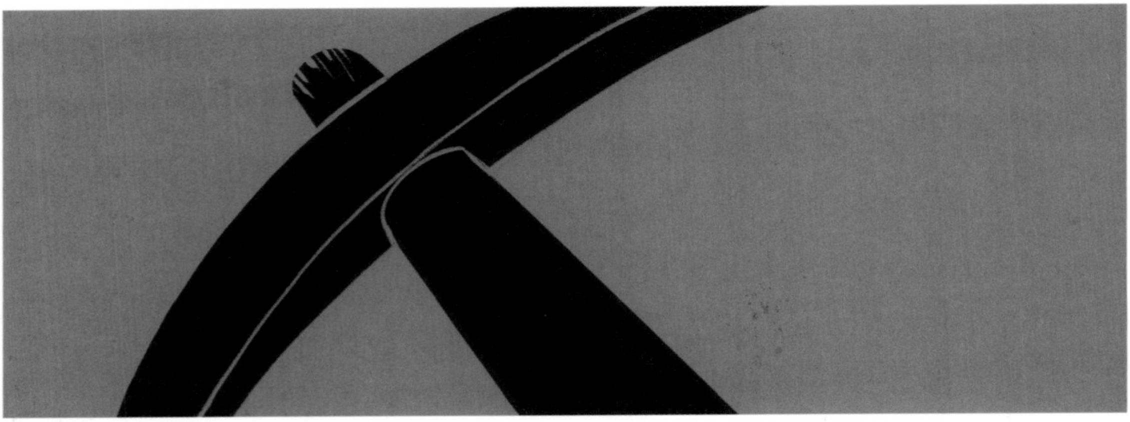

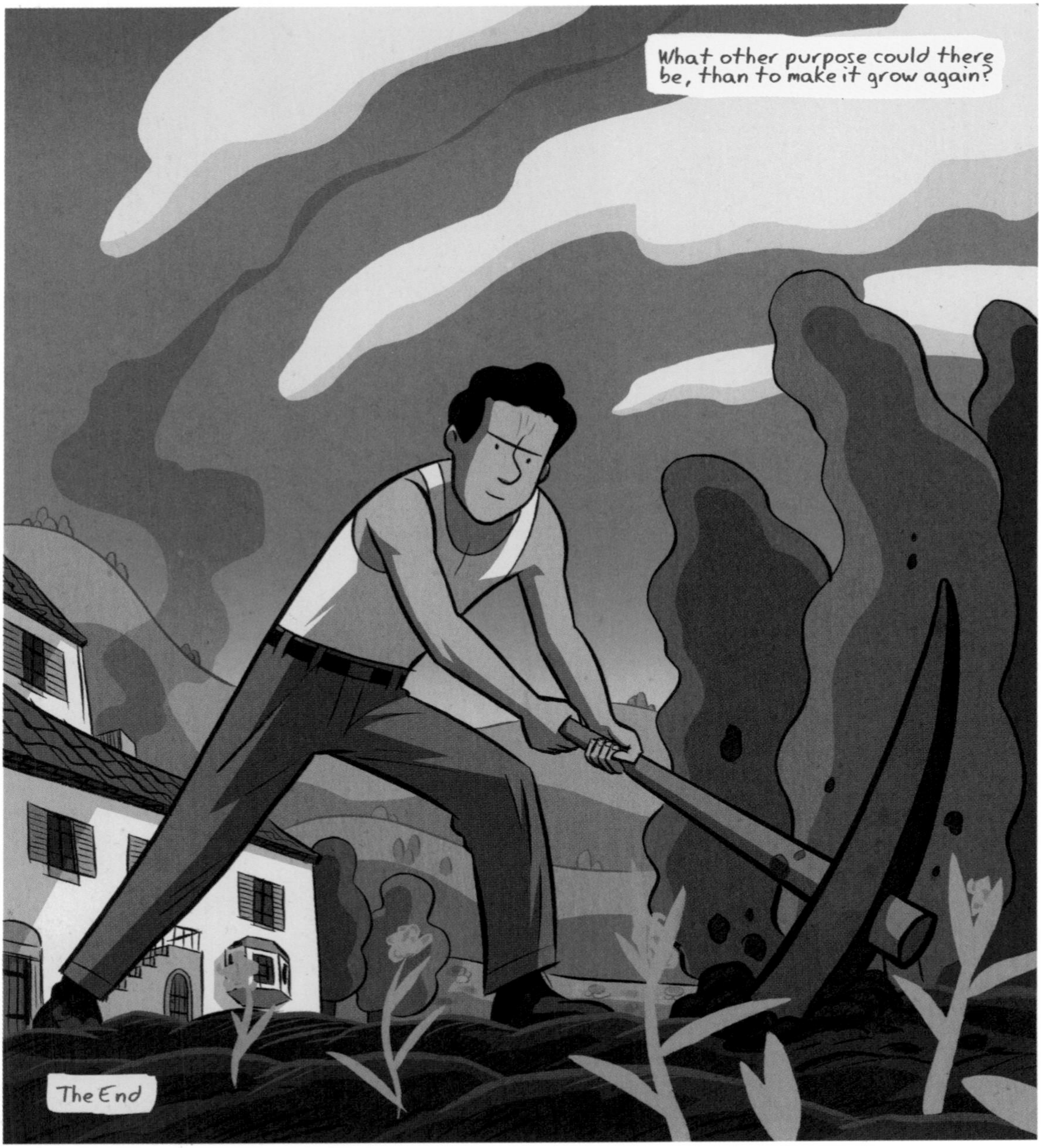
What other purpose could there be, than to make it grow again?
The End

Epilogue

In 1943, after the fall of the Italian Fascist Party, Paolo's case was reopened. This was largely due to the efforts of Gaetano Sardiello, who had been the lead defending attorney twenty years earlier.

For the first time, the eyewitnesses who had been kept from testifying in the original trial were given a chance to speak on record.

Paolo's conviction was overturned, and Gato was sentenced to 25 years in prison.

Parade (with fireworks) is dedicated
in loving memory of
SILVIO GIORGIO TEGANINI
1945 – 2007

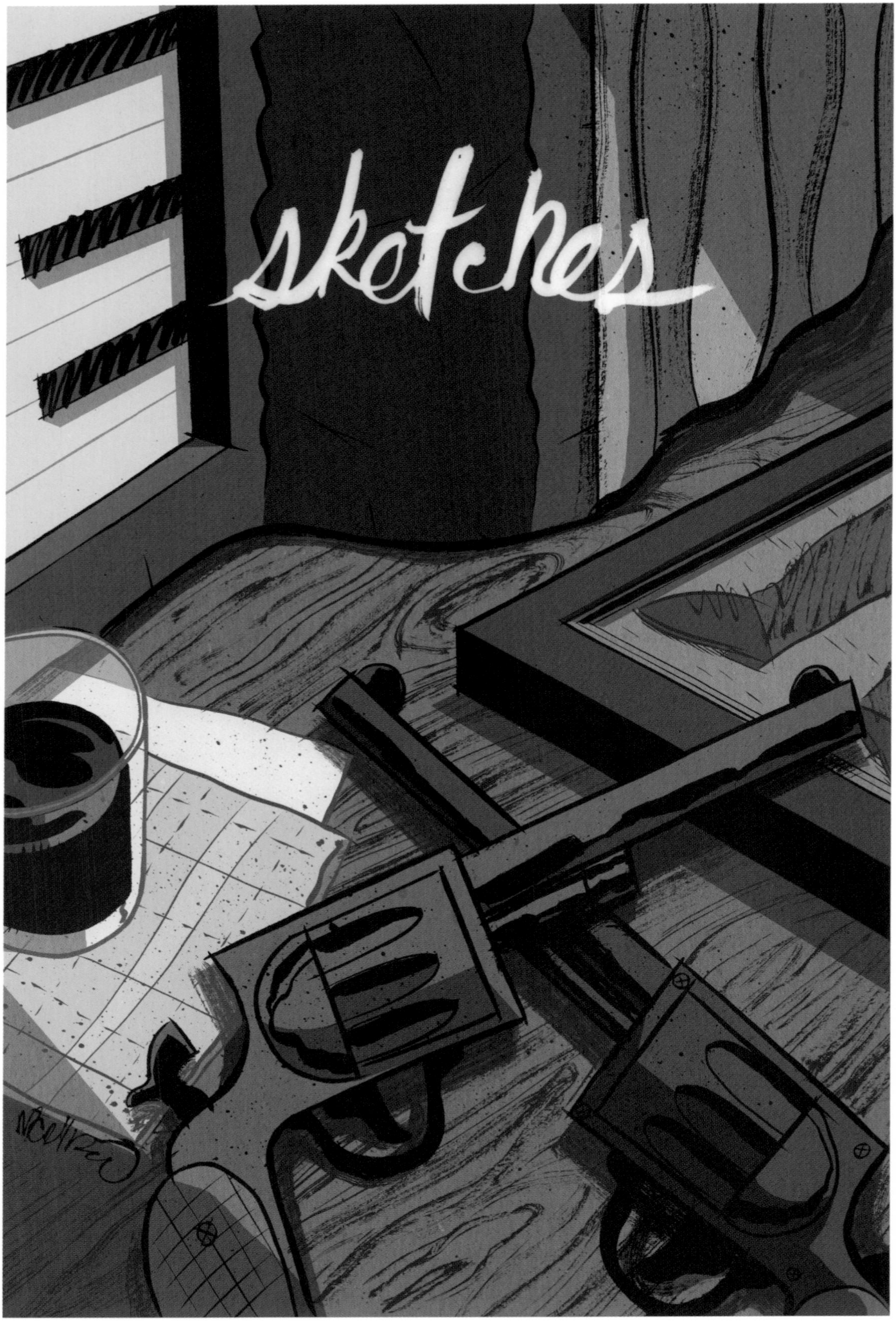
sketches

AFTERWORD

y Dean Haspiel

d met Mike Cavallaro a handful of times at various local comix vents but we never took it beyond a cordial handshake and hello." He looked a lot like a rockabilly-punk version of actor, teve Buscemi, but more like a scrappy Italian reject from he T-Birds in the movie, RE ASE.

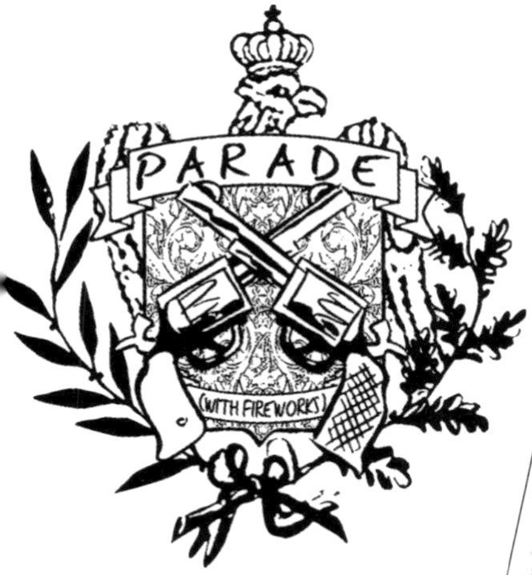
PARADE
(WITH FIREWORKS)

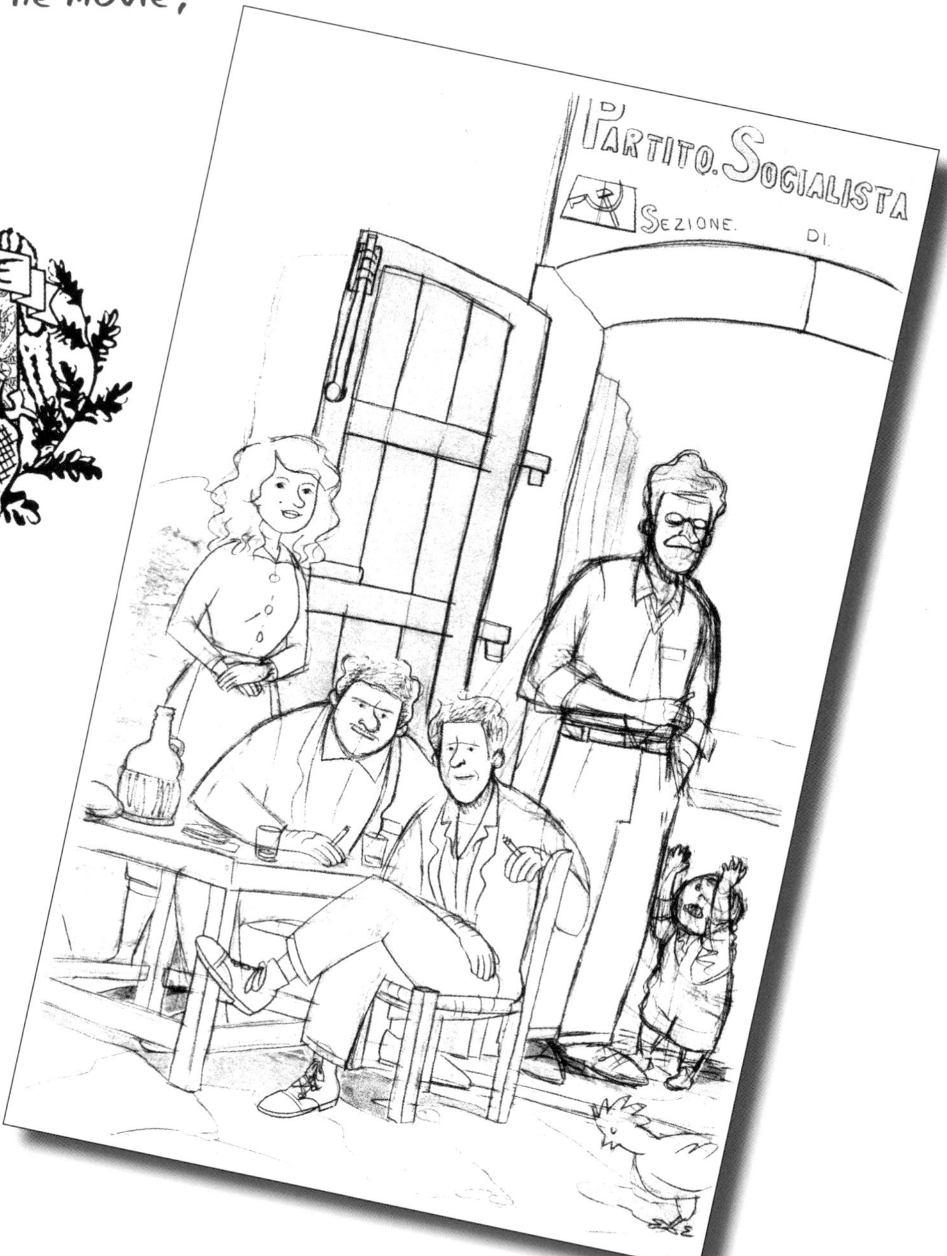
PARTITO. SOCIALISTA
SEZIONE. DI.

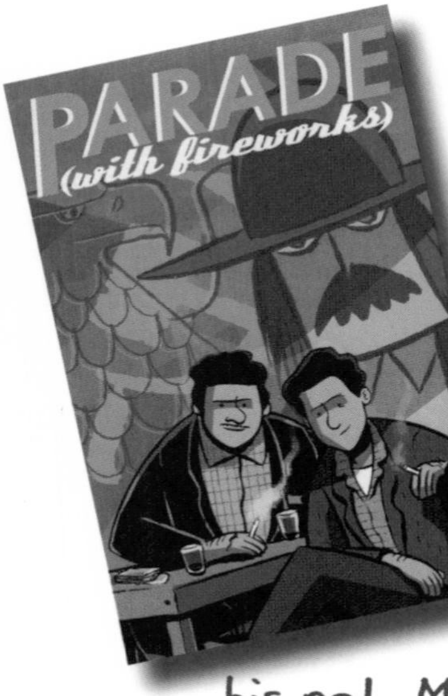
PARADE
(with fireworks)

It was Tim Hamilton who cornered Mike Cavallaro and brought him into the fray. Tim is a co-founder of ACT-I-VATE, the premiere webcomix initiative I launched in February of 2006 with a select group of cartoonists, and he needed to go on hiatus to complete a paying gig. Tim's hiatus would last no more than a couple of months and he suggested that his pal, Mike, could fill his spot on the weekly schedule until his return. We weren't adverse to guests and, if Tim said Mike was okay, then Mike was okay. So we gave the new guy th greenlight and a couple of weeks later, Parade (with Fireworks debuted at ACT-I-VATE. Eyes popped and the comments section of our webcomix blog started to fill with high-praise and cheer for the new guy. By the third installment, Cavallaro was no longer a guest but a crucial member of our elite and a publisher was already soliciting him. Before Parade was halfway finished, Kristen Simon and Jim Valentino had the foresight to recognize a great comic book in the making and Mike signed with Shadowline to publish a two-issue, Eisner Award nominated mini-series version of the final tome you now hold in your hands.

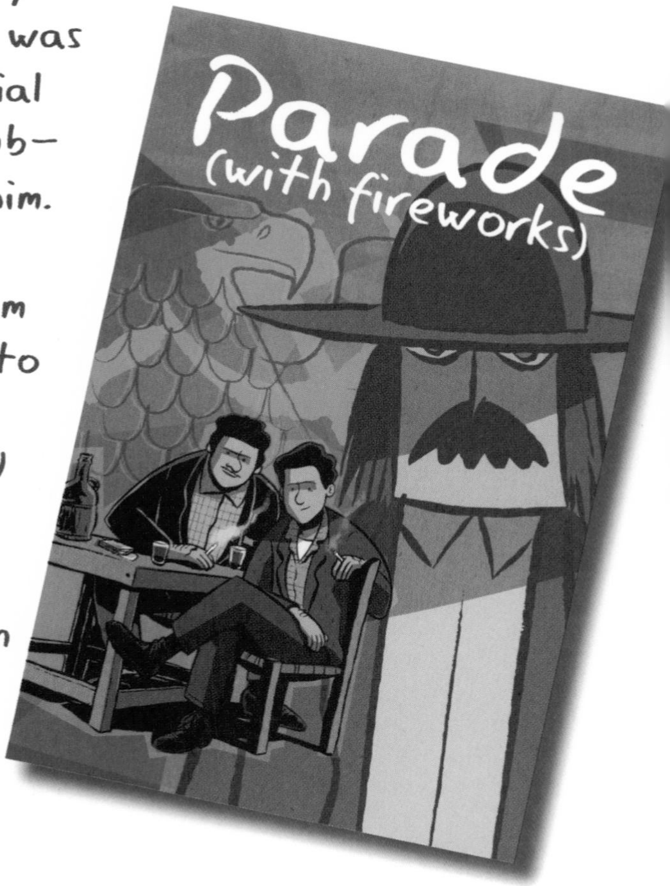
Parade
(with fireworks)

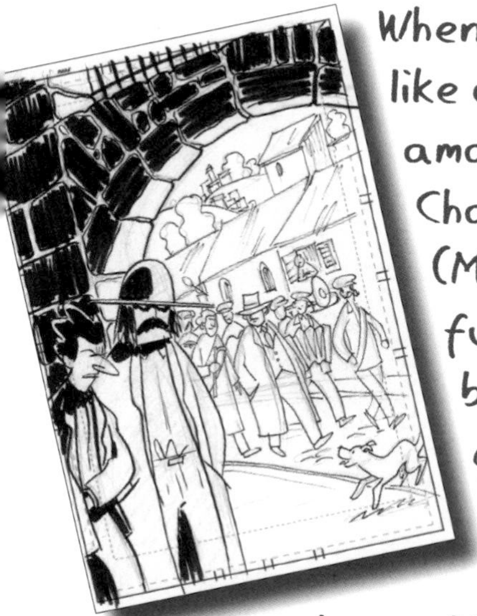

When I first saw Parade, I thought it looked like an elegant yet action-oriented amalgamation of the best works of Yves Chaland (SPIROU) and Dupuy & Berberian (MONSIEUR JEAN). Cavallaro's purposefully "Ligne claire" art style was informed by his animation background yet boosted by his thick brush strokes and was made manifest by his seductive

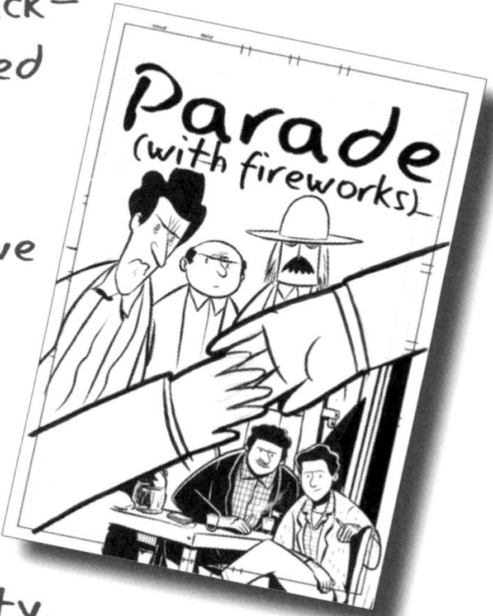
Parade
(with fireworks)

oloring. Mike's pacing and storytelling as intelligent and entertaining yet the ctual tale was one I'd never seen nor read in comix before, told with utmost respect and sensitivity.

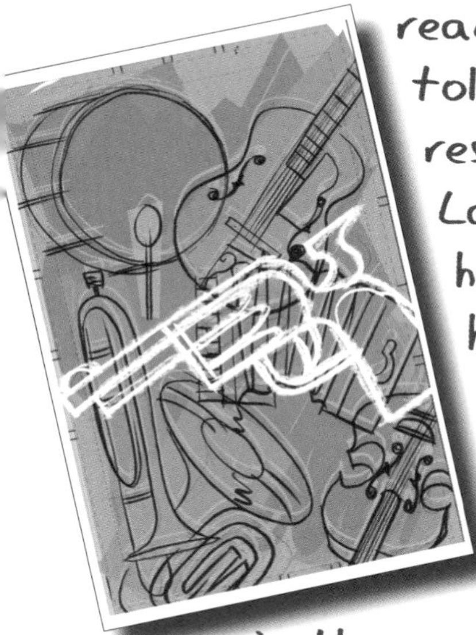

Later on, Mike would admit to me that he employed this new style to break old habits. I was floored by Mike's talent, professionalism, and commitment to stay on schedule, a code rarely accomplished in the comix industry, today.

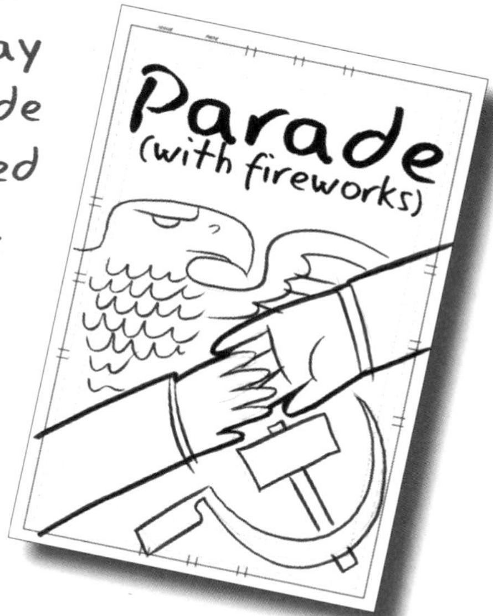
Parade
(with fireworks)

Come Spring 2007, "Cav" became my nickname for Mike Cavallaro, shortly after he and I and four other highly talented cartoonist formed DEEP6 Studios in Gowanus, Brooklyn. A place for us to escape the loneliness of our home studios and make comix among each other. Despite his heartfelt admiration for his hometown hero, Bruce Springsteen, Cav shared hilarious war stories about his tenure at Valiant Comics while providing endless anecdotes about his days playing music and touring with his band, STICKS AND STONES, and with his pals, THE BOUNCING SOULS. And, not unlike some of the lessons imparted by the tragic events in Parade, I learned a lot from Cav during ping pong breaks and late night shifts eating peanut butter and jelly sandwiches at DEEP6 about what made people tick and how to better realize and exploit the virtues of a studio and webcomix collective. I came to count on Cav and call him my friend.

arade came to its eventual conclusion and Cav started working n FOILED, an original, young adult, graphic novel written by ane Yolen for First Second Books. While tackling freelance work, av curiously entrenched himself in Stan Lee and Jack Kirby's ntire run on THOR, declaring issue #136, "the greatest comic ook ever made," while studying Will Eisner's THE SPIRIT and ketch books, and Milton Caniff's STEVE CANYON. I could see he wheels turning in Cav's head and I knew he was steeping in his particular trio of comix masters for his sophomore opus. fter much cajoling, I challenged Cav to write and draw his ersion of his favorite DC Comics superhero, AQUAMAN. See, Cav as disgruntled with the fact that AQUAMAN always got the hort shrift and DC hadn't figured out a way to keep he "King of Atlantis" in regular rotation. I can't take the redit for what happened next but few weeks later I saw Cav drawing urky images of fish and underwater reatures in battle gear and there ere explosions. Later that night, received an email from Cav that tated his new strip for ACT-I-VATE ould be called LOVIATHAN, with a easer that declared, "Love is the nd of the World." I think it took whole week before publishers and riters came knocking down Cav's oor.

—Dean Haspiel
reator of BILLY DOGMA) NYC 2008

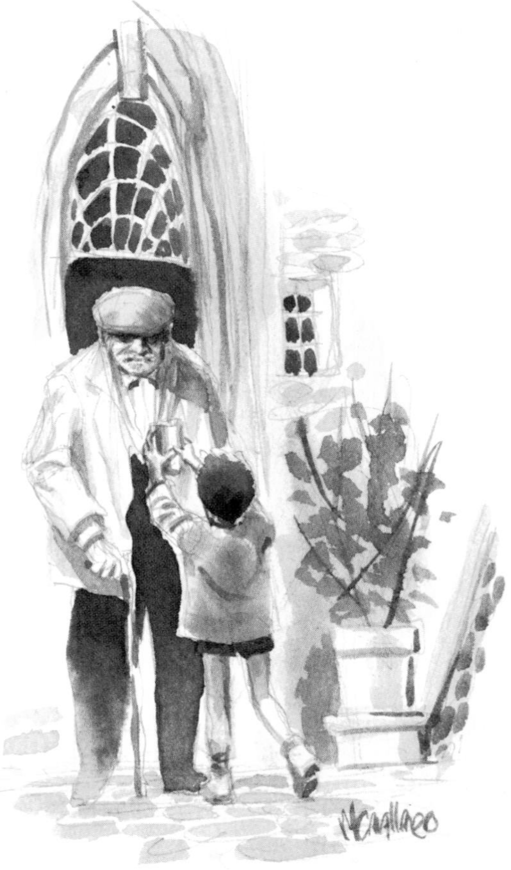

ACKNOWLEDGEMENTS

In the 60's my parents and grandparents moved to the U.S. from southern Italy. They brought a lot of stories with them about what it was like growing up there in the first half of the century. These were vivid and revealing tales, and seemed to hint at a rich and ancient world that had been lost somehow between the two World Wars.

At some point I decided to start writing them down.

My mom says I made a lot of changes, but the challenge of reconstructing a story like this brings with it nuances and complexities I hadn't expected. It's been a learning experience. In the end, I didn't want the tale's basis in reality to be the best thing it had going for it. I wasn't sure the fact that it actually happened could make up for an unsatisfying read, or for failing to make readers care about the story.

Whatever fine-tuning I applied I feel was necessary since, among other things, I was left to ponder the actions of people who's motivations have been lost in the ensuing decades. Normally, I asked myself, "Why would *I* do that?" I tried to be as sympathetic to all parties as I could.

I see Parade as a strange little vignette, hovering between fact and fiction, a quick fade-in and fade-out on a small puzzle piece of my own history, and maybe an even smaller puzzle piece in a larger history. It definitely filled-in some gaps for me, and I hope in some way it does the same for some readers.

Many thanks go out to my mom and dad, Georgina and Francesco Cavallaro, for years of love, support and encouragement. Thanks also to Lisa Natoli, Ann Marie Winchock, Paul Cavallaro, Tim Hamilton, Dean Haspiel, Joan Reilly, Leland Purvis, Simon Fraser, Michel Fiffe, Joe Infurnari, Nathan Schreiber, J.M. DeMatteis, Mark Siegel, Gina Gagliano, Nick Bertozzi, Dan Goldman, Jeff Newelt, Seth Kushner, Martin Cuevas, and to all of ACT-I-VATE.com, including the readers that followed Parade from its online beginnings.

Thank you, Scott Friedlander, without whom I couldn't have assembled this book nearly as well.

Special thanks go out to Kristen Simon and Jim Valentino at Shadowline Comics, who believed in my project enough to see it through to print, for which I'm eternally grateful. Thank you, as well, to Joe Keatinge, Traci Hui, Allen Hui, and Erik Larsen at Image Comics.

Mike Cavallaro

PLEASE VISIT: www.activatecomix.com   www.mikecavallaro.com

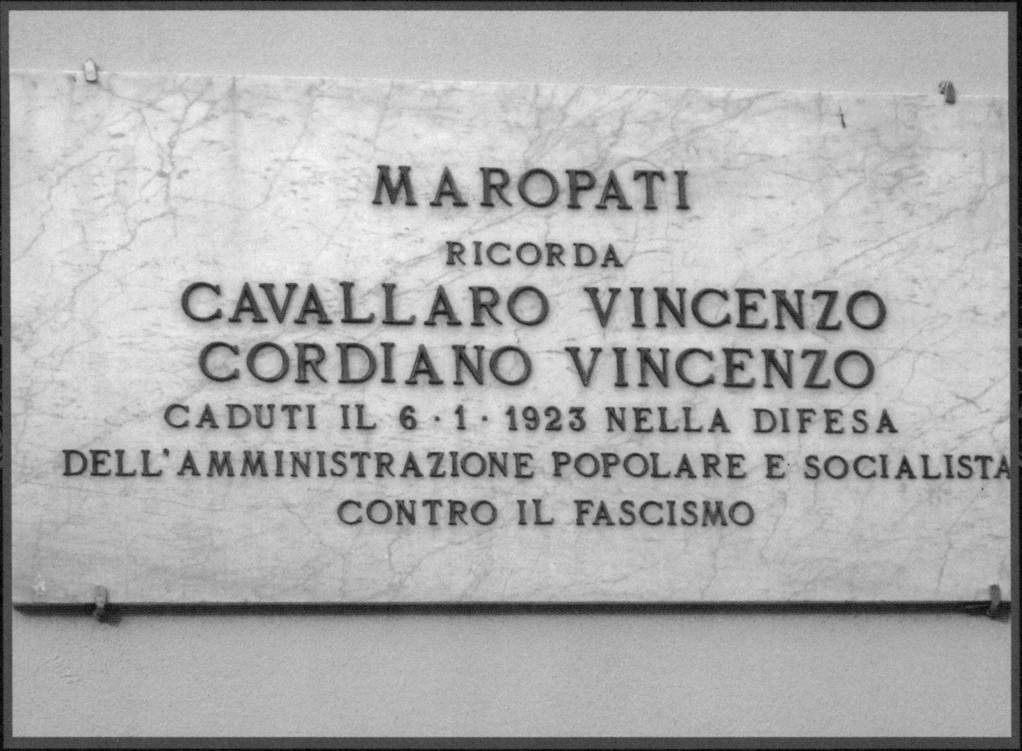
MAROPATI
RICORDA
CAVALLARO VINCENZO
CORDIANO VINCENZO
CADUTI IL 6 · 1 · 1923 NELLA DIFESA
DELL'AMMINISTRAZIONE POPOLARE E SOCIALISTA
CONTRO IL FASCISMO

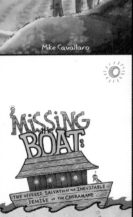

GRAPHIC NOVELS

ACCELERATE
KARDREY, PANDER BROTHERS

AFTER THE CAPE: HOW FAR TO FALL
WONG, VALENTINO, RUDY

AFTER THE CAPE II: ALL FALLS DOWN
WONG, VALENTINO, CARRERA

BOMB QUEEN: WMD
JIMMIE ROBINSON

BOMB QUEEN II: DIRTY BOMB
JIMMIE ROBINSON

BOMB QUEEN III: BOMBSHELL
JIMMIE ROBINSON

BOMB QUEEN IV: SUICIDE BOMBER
JIMMIE ROBINSON

BRUCE: THE LITTLE BLUE SPRUCE
SIMON, VALENTINO

COMPLETE normalman
VALENTINO

DEAR DRACULA
WILLIAMSON, NAVARETTE

DNAGENTS
EVANIER, MEUGNIOT

MISSING THE BOAT
SHADY, WELLEPHANT

NEW WORLD ORDER: DAWN OF A NEW DAY
HIGUERA, FERRERYA and FRIENDS

PARADE (WITH FIREWORKS)
CAVALLARO

PX! A GIRL AND HER PANDA
TREMBELEY, ANDERSON

SAM NOIR VOLUME ONE
TREMBELEY, ANDERSON

SURREAL ADVENTURES OF EDGAR ALLAN POO
MacPHERSON, BOATWRIGHT

SURREAL ADVENTURES OF EDGAR ALLAN POO II
MacPHERSON, BUTTERWORTH

TRANSIT
TED McKEEVER

UNEARTHED CEMETERY BLUES
RUBIO, BOATWRIGHT

VIGNETTES
VALENTINO